Performance Literacy through Storytelling

Nile Stanley and Brett Dillingham

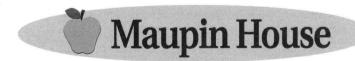

Maupin House

Performance Literacy through Storytelling
© 2009 Nile Stanley and Brett Dillingham. All Rights Reserved.
Reproducible pages in this resource may be duplicated for single-classroom use only.

Cover, book design, and layout: Studio Montage

Library of Congress Cataloging-in-Publication Data

Stanley, Nile, 1954-
  Performance literacy through storytelling / Nile Stanley and Brett
Dillingham.
    p. cm.
  Includes bibliographical references and index.
  ISBN-13: 978-1-934338-41-4 (pbk.)
  ISBN-10: 1-934338-41-9 (pbk.)
  1. Storytelling. 2. Early childhood education–Activity programs. I.
Dillingham, Brett. II. Title.
  LB1042.S73 2009
  372.67'7–dc22
                              2009008622

Thanks to the following for permission to use and reprint the copyrighted materials listed below:

KAREN ALEXANDER. "October 31st" and "Blizzard Wizard" from *Fly Away Fall*, 2002, by Karen Alexander, Entertain Reading. "The Sleeping Sea" and "The UnderToe" from *Once Upon a Seaside*, 2003, by Karen Alexander. http://www.abcpoet-tree.com/

JOHN ARCHAMBAULT, BILL MARTIN JR., and DAVID PLUMMER. "Barn Dance," 2003. From *Barn Dance* (CD), by Bill Martin Jr. and John Archambault. Henry Holt and Company, 1988. http://www.johnarchambault.com/

BEN BRENNER arranged music and played guitar and percussion on "How Drum Learned to Talk" by Nile Stanley; "October 31st," "Blizzard Wizard," "The UnderToe," and "The Sleeping Sea" by Karen Alexander; and "Spudbuster" by Nile Stanley and Ben Brenner. www.myspace.com/mr_the_ben

HEATHER FOREST. "The Little Red Hen," composed and performed by Heather Forest from *Sing Me A Story*. Recording is used with permission from A Gentle Wind, Box 3103, Albany, NY 12203. www.gentlewind.com • www.storyarts.org.

BRENDA HOLLINGSWORTH-MARLEY. "Hummingbird and Elephant," retold for this book. http://professionalstoryteller.ning.com/profile/BrendaHollingsworthMarley

JASON OHLER. "Digital Storytelling Mini-Lesson: Two Stories about Ourselves," written for this book. www.jasonohler.com/

JOY STEINER. "Boreal Owlets," written for this book. www.joysteiner.com.

JEFF TRIPPE. "I'm a Jinx," written for this book. http://cdbaby.com/cd/trippejeff

ALLAN WOLF. "Patrick Gas, the Carpenter," excerpted from *New Found Land: Lewis and Clark's Voyage of Discovery* (pp.77–78). Copyright © Allan Wolf. Reproduced by permission of the publisher, Candlewick Press, Somerville, MA. http://www.allanwolf.com/

ISBN-13: 978-1-934338-41-4

Contact Maupin House for tailored, in-school training or to schedule an author for a workshop or conference. Visit www.maupinhouse.com for free lesson plan downloads.

Maupin House Publishing, Inc.
2416 NW 71 Place • Gainesville, FL 32653
www.maupinhouse.com • info@maupinhouse.com
800-524-0634 / 352-373-5588 (phone) • 352-373-5546 (fax)

10 9 8 7 6 5 4 3 2 1

Dedication

"Myths are clues to the spiritual potentialities of the human life."
"The big question is whether you are going to be able to say a hearty yes to your adventure."
Joseph Campbell, *The Power of Myth*

Thanks to Heather Forest, Bill Martin Jr., John Archambault, David Plummer, Allan Wolf, Joy Steiner, Ben Brenner, Karen Alexander, and Brenda Hollingsworth-Marley for their contributions to and performances on the audio CD included with this book.

From Nile

I hadn't planned to meet storyteller Brett Dillingham in Indianapolis in 2000, but I did and that has made all the difference. You had the courage to follow your bliss, do what is best for humanity, children, schools and community. Thanks for teaching me the magic and power of performance literacy. I dedicate this book to you and all the other myth makers: Karen Alexander, John Archambault, Ben Brenner, Heather Forest, Brenda Hollingsworth-Marley, Bill Martin Jr., Jason Ohler, David Plummer, Joy Steiner, Jeff Trippe, and Allan Wolf. Thanks to all those who love learning, literacy, music, poetry, and storytelling, and who inspired and supported me: Cheryl and Jack of the Cummer Family Foundation; Larry Daniel, Pat Hanford, and the Foundation of the University of North Florida; the teachers, Steffanie Gilligan and Vivianne Davis, and all the children and parents; my wife, Dr. Laurel, critical theorist, and daughter Jane, guitar hero and digital storyteller.

From Brett

Thanks to my mother Beth Dillingham and grandmother Una Wilder for nurturing the stories within me; to Susan Hanson, whose mentorship in literacy was a gift I try to pass on; to Mark Whitman, talented storyteller and the true "Dr Amiesenhaufen"; Dr. Jason Ohler, friend, visionary, anthropologist, and the finest digital storytelling instructor on the planet. Gracious thanks as well to Christine McMahon, wonderful storyteller and youth advocate in Calderdale, England; Liz Morris, teacher extraordinaire in Dublin, Ireland; and Ann Symons, librarian empress of Russia. Miceal Ross, friend, storyteller, and Renaissance man from Monkstown, Ireland, told me more tales than I have ever read. Marion Healy of Cork, Ireland for sharing her wonderful students year after year. Simone MacHamer, for her friendship and gracious support working with Irish children of poverty and Alaska Natives; to Sghen-doo George, Tlingit Indian teacher and artist. Linda Perez, Janice Ferdinand, and Veronica Prescott for their warmth and professionalism working with their students in St. Croix. Karin Halpin, reading expert and co-worker, who helped me work with the Yupik Eskimo. All the caring, sharing teachers who let me introduce performance literacy and storytelling to their incredible students. Thanks to Nile Stanley, co-author of this book, for being that rare professor who "walks the walk," working with real children and in such an extraordinary way. Finally, thanks to my wife Kristy Dillingham for her being such a wonderful mother to our children, wife to me, and for her constant support and encouragement.

Table of Contents

PART I: Storytelling Strategies, Stages, and Structure

The first half of this book lays out the basics you'll need to make storytelling a part of your classroom using the performance literacy approach.

provides all the background information you need to know about storytelling, its conventions, how it develops literacy, and how you can fit it into the language arts block and your busy day.

addresses the first component of storytelling—story development—and provides instructions on teaching beginning, intermediate, and advanced storytelling mini-lessons using the standards-based performance literacy framework.

discusses the second component of storytelling—story delivery—and provides easy-to-follow tips, games, and rubrics to help you improve and evaluate your students' performances.

PART II: The Mini-lessons

The *how* and *what* of each of the three stages of storytelling—beginning, intermediate, and advanced—are provided within the mini-lesson chapters in the second half of this book. You know your students best. You should decide when they are ready to advance to the next storytelling stage and in what areas they need more work.

Introduction

Come in! Come in! Would you like to hear a story? It's Friday afternoon and there are more than 300 students, teachers, and parents gathered in the school gymnasium. There is a line of children eager to perform the stories they have written about Alaskan animals. Pamela, a smiling, animated, and confident fourth grader begins.

"It was a foggy day and the wind was blowing. It was the day of the Iditarod, the great sled race. All the dogs were ready. But Musher, the dog who always lost, was determined to win. Then, BANG! The starter's gun fired, and off they went…"

Across the ocean, a similar gathering of "yarn spinners" takes place in a British school. Kids are enjoying themselves; getting up in front of their peers, teachers, and communities; and engaging in literate behavior. One particular "star," David, is a boy who, up to this storytelling performance, had been withdrawn and disruptive, seldom participating in speaking, reading, or writing. When asked by his teacher if he needed help telling the story, David replied, "No, I want to do it myself."

During our combined forty years of teaching children around the world—from remote Alaskan Native villages, international schools in different countries and Irish working-class towns to American inner cities and inclusive suburbs— we observe a universal truth. Children love to tell stories if we provide encouragement and take the time to listen. A lesser known truth is that storytelling can be part of the daily curriculum, prompting powerful lessons about language and literacy.

Traditionally, storytelling has had a very limited role in classrooms and is most often used for entertainment. It occurs in a school or language arts classroom perhaps once or twice a year, if at all. Teachers might invite a storyteller to perform at a school-wide assembly. Maybe students are asked to create a story based on the American Indian unit they're working on in class. Without adequate time to rehearse, many of the students choose not to tell the story. They are too shy, feel embarrassed, or don't think their story/storytelling is "good enough."

In contrast to more traditional storytelling applications in schools, the performance literacy process uses storytelling to develop all components of literacy, encouraging both academic and social growth that is accessible to all students. Simply put, performance literacy is the process of teaching students to write and perform stories. But the phrase, coined by Brett Dillingham (2005), encompasses much more. Performance literacy is a powerful educational approach that increases students' language development, vocabulary, and comprehension; internalizes an understanding of the writing process; integrates learning across the content areas; develops speaking and listening skills; and deepens the connection between home, school, and community.

Through performance literacy,

- students are taught to consciously use sound, expression, and movement to tell stories with an impact.
- story ideas are elicited from the students themselves, supporting the use of prior knowledge, a critical component of writing and motivation.
- students tell and retell stories to one another before turning in a written first draft. This provides a safe environment in which students verbally create and "fill in" their stories.
- students are taught how to critique each other in a non-threatening manner, encouraging respect while providing suggestions for improvement.
- final performances, with a real audience of other classes, parents, and often community members, are a much more satisfying way to showcase students' abilities than telling stories to just their own classmates.

This practical guide is for busy K–8 teachers who want to know how to use storytelling to motivate and engage reluctant readers and writers. Mini-lessons at beginning, intermediate, and advanced levels help teachers weave storytelling into the fabric of today's standards-based classroom and construct their own skillful literacy lessons.

Why Teach Storytelling?

The development of children's language skills begins at birth, and children become more proficient with language by using it. Adult interaction with children through conversation, play, reading aloud, and storytelling are essential in early childhood education. Children of all ages, especially the very young, learn through contextually rich stories.

Research indicates that children's school success is highly influenced by the frequency of listening to stories read to them. Children under four who tell and hear stories at home are most likely to learn to read easily and with interest once they get to school. By age eight, most children can tell a well-formed narrative. Our minds are literally wired to comprehend reality through stories. We make sense of our lives by organizing life's events in the story format.

Children's storytelling skill development evolves, too, proceeding through five levels: labeling, listing, connecting, sequencing, and narrating. The early phases of young children's narrative development revolve around conversations about immediate, familiar objects. For example, in labeling and listing, a child points and says, "That is a fish. That is a blue one. That is a gold one." Later, through adult-centered activities, especially with books, children become more sophisticated. They are able to tell more abstract stories about imagined events from the past in which they connect, sequence, and narrate, such as retelling a familiar folk tale, for example.

For children to become literate storytellers who can connect, sequence, and narrate, caregivers and teachers must provide encouragement and multiple opportunities to experience language from different venues. Children must learn to write and tell their own stories.

When children have opportunities to perform their own stories, they often develop an increased interest in writing, reading, listening, and speaking. Children who tell stories learn to put their own voice down on paper. By retelling and rereading their stories again and again, children develop reading, oral and listening fluency. They begin reading like they speak and speaking like they read.

The National Reading Panel (NRP) advocates a comprehensive approach to literacy education, calling for instruction in five areas and informally known as the "five pillars of effective reading instruction": phonemic awareness, phonics, fluency, vocabulary, and comprehension—along with early and continued exposure to rich literature and writing opportunities. Performance literacy supports a much more comprehensive literacy approach. Too often in the zeal to teach skills and prepare students for high-stakes tests, teachers don't use storytelling properly or to its full potential. A comprehensive literacy approach requires more than just teaching the skills. With storytelling you can meet standards-based expectations while also developing imagination, fostering powerful communication, and motivating students to step outside of their comfort zone.

The International Reading Association (IRA) and the National Council of Teachers of English (NCTE) advocate that teachers tap into the power of storytelling. Although educators know that oral-language development is the most important foundation and component of reading and writing, often not enough is provided to stimulate early literacy growth. Older students have better retention when content knowledge—in science and history, for example—is delivered as a story.

State standards always involve building reading, writing, speaking, and listening skills. These skills are naturally embedded within storytelling, improving students' literacy skills and, subsequently, their test scores.

Teachers from around the world have tried our methods for developing literacy skills through storytelling in their international or national standards-based curriculums, and the results speak for themselves. Storytelling
- increases opportunities for writing.
- develops self-expression and confidence.
- is accessible to all children and easy to use in any class.
- forges positive home/school connections.
- works across the content areas to make subjects come alive.
- builds engagement and enjoyment in reading while building reading skills.
- supports standards and raises test scores.
- helps English-language and striving learners acquire language, vocabulary, and listening skills.

It does not matter if teachers work mostly with mainstream students or with students from high-poverty situations, in special education classes, or with behavior problems. The performance literacy approach works well with children who aren't expected to engage in high-achieving social and academic behavior because it allows any child to experience success. Storytelling changes the expectations of both students and their teachers for the better.

Once students hear a good story and understand that good storytelling involves using sound, expression, and movement, they see how easy it is to create a visual portrait of a story. Then they can produce their own stories and realize how accessible this literacy art is to everyone, including themselves. Once students tell their story to a real audience, they learn to believe in themselves because they have accomplished something significant and challenging. As children gain confidence with telling and writing their own stories, they advance their communication abilities by connecting and collaborating with the literate community. Students learn to create stories from stories by modeling the language patterns of the rich traditional literature of folktales and children's books they read, study, and retell.

What You Will Find in This Book

All of the stories and teaching strategies in this book have been field-tested with children, educators, parents, and diverse communities. Included in the field testing were three predominately African-American magnet schools for the performing arts in Jacksonville, Florida. In these schools, pre-service and experienced teachers used storytelling strategies to teach reading and language arts methods classes. Field testing also included students in remote Alaskan villages; poor neighborhoods in Ireland and England, International schools in Europe, Asia, and Africa; and the inner-city "hoods" and barrios of America. Storytelling is particularly valuable in print-poor environments, where children have limited access to books.

This resource includes:
- **Full-length stories** and useful excerpts by premier authors for reader's theater, storytelling, and skill development, selected as excellent read-aloud models. Many educators, storytellers, and performers contributed their work to this book.
    - ➤ **Karen Alexander** is a children's author, poet, and published storyteller (*Chicken Soup for the Soul*) who masterfully combines rhyme, rhythm, and repetition for enthralling audiences.
    - ➤ **John Archambault**, award-winning author of *Chicka Chicka Boom Boom*, and **David Plummer**, British recording artist, use melody and song to carry words along in foot-stomping storytelling and story-dancing.
    - ➤ **Ben Brenner**, a performance educator, is a heavy metal recording artist who is in the storytelling duo ER—Entertain Reading with Nile Stanley.
    - ➤ **Brett Dillingham** offers storytelling at its best—timeless and entertaining with the tone of campfire intimacy and the drama of theatre. His original folktales of wonder, trickery, and adventure enthrall with his rich vocal collection of animal sounds and other interesting effects.
    - ➤ **Heather Forest**, award-winning recording artist, offers a unique minstrel style of storytelling, blending folk guitar, prose, and poetry.
    - ➤ **Brenda Hollingsworth-Marley**, "the Storybird," specializes in African-American tales and is an exuberant, spirit-filled performer, librarian, actress, dancer, drummer, and vocalist.
    - ➤ **Jason Ohler** is a speaker, writer, teacher, researcher, and one of the foremost authorities on digital storytelling.

- ➤ **Nile Stanley**, "Nile Crocodile, the Reading Reptile," is a professor, poet, musician, and digital storyteller, who teaches literacy and literacy educators through the arts.
- ➤ **Joy Steiner** tells nature stories with a sense of adventure. She has leapt into icy, high-mountain lakes green with glacier dust and snorkeled with barracuda in the warm gulf waters of Mexico.
- ➤ **Jeff Trippe** is a musician, educator, and freelance writer. He lives in Yarmouth, Maine, with his wife, Laura, and daughter, Alex.
- ➤ **Allan Wolf** is an author, poet, performer and past education director for Poetry Alive! Allan's writing has earned many honors, including a *School Library Journal* Best Book.

- **Highly engaging, standards-based mini-lessons** focusing on the essential literacy skills for beginning, intermediate, and advanced levels.
- **Research-informed teaching strategies, activities, and tools** for developing literacy through storytelling.
- **A 70-minute CD of stories and songs** performed by renowned storytellers for encouraging performance and multimedia learning, such as digital storytelling.
- **Information for using the companion website** at http://www.unf.edu/ ~nstanley/links.htm, with supporting videos, articles, mini-lessons, and resources.
- **A list of resources** for optimizing success with reading, writing, and performing stories; assessment tools; and connections to traditional folk literature and relevant children's books.

Storytellers and their stories are diverse, but all good storytellers use the same foundational skills and strategies found in this book. We want children to know that they can write and perform their own stories. We want them to know what a story is and what it looks like when written down and acted out. Most importantly, we want children to master the valuable life skill of communicating through story. Communication is all about stories.

PART I

Storytelling Strategies, Stages, and Structure

Chapter 1

Storytelling Develops Literacy

Since ancient times, stories have been shared in every culture and in every land as a means to educate, entertain, preserve culture, and instill knowledge, values, and morals. Stories, with their plots, characters, and narrative point of view, use words, pictures, and acting to teach, explain, and entertain.

Traditional Literature

Folktales are the mother of all literature. The foundation of storytelling builds upon traditional literature, stories, poems, and songs about the struggles of ordinary people or the common folk. These folktales represent a great, ancient, oral tradition containing centuries of accumulated wisdom. They were initially told and later written down, so very few have known, identifiable authors. There is no one definitive version of a piece of folk literature because stories were modified as various tellers passed them along orally. For example, there are hundreds of versions (referred to as *variant tales*) of the *Cinderella* story across many cultures. The stories all focus on the struggles of everyday life.

Although the terms *folktale* and *fairy tale* are often used interchangeably, the fairy tale is really a type of folktale with magic characters. Some time in the late 1200s a collection of 181 folk tales and anecdotes called the *Gesta Romanorum* was compiled. The Brothers Grimm and Hans Christian Andersen were some of the first to systematically collect and record written tales of the common people. *Grimm's Fairy Tales* (1812) are enduring classics like *Snow White, Hansel and Gretel*, and *Rapunzel.* Andersen's (1835) *Fairy Tales* include the immortal *The Ugly Duckling, The Little Mermaid*, and *The Princess and the Pea.*

Knowledge about traditional literature is a very important part of understanding the way that children develop their storytelling skills. Many children's literature textbooks provide a comprehensive discussion of the traditional literature genre with lists of story anthologies and picture-book adaptations. Traditional tales are broadly categorized as cumulative, humorous, beast, magic, pourquoi, and realistic. These categories often overlap. Additional information on the various types of stories and characteristic elements are addressed where appropriate in this book's mini-lessons, and an index of suggested stories by category is found at the end of this book. Lynch-Brown and Tomlinson's *Essentials of Children's Literature* (2005) discusses the most prevalent kinds of folktales summarized here.

- **Cumulative tales** are often rhythmic and use a bare-bones plot, repetition, and accumulation to tell an entertaining story ("The Three Little Pigs," "There Was an Old Lady Who Swallowed a Fly," "The House That Jack Built," and "The Little Red Hen," which is a musical cumulative tale).

- **Humorous tales, noodlehead stories, or trickster tales** are about a silly or stupid person who nevertheless wins out in the end (*Lazy Jack*, *Brer Rabbit*, and *Anansi the Spider*).
- **Talking beast stories or fables** are tales where animals can talk just like people. Generally, they are didactic and show the results of bravery, self-reliance, and resourcefulness ("The Things Willy Wumperbill Saw," "The Three Billy Goats Gruff," and "The Little Red Hen").
- **Magic tales or fairy tales** contain elements of magic or enchantment in characters, plot, or setting. Fairies, wizards, witches, flying carpets, magic lamps, and enchanted forests are common in these stories ("Little Red Riding Hood," "Sleeping Beauty," and "Aladdin and the Wonderful Lamp").
- **Porquoi or creation tales** explain phenomena of nature. The word *porquoi* is French for *why*: *Why do the sun and moon live in the sky? Why do mosquitoes buzz in people's ears?*
- **Realistic stories** deal with characters, plots, and exaggeration, but no talking animals, magic castles, or flying carpets are involved ("Dick Whittington and His Cat" and "Bluebeard").

There are, of course, many more types of traditional literature including ballads, epics, legends, Mother Goose tales, myths, religious tales, romances, and story poems. Modern folklorists continue to collect the tales, urban legends, ghost stories, jokes, and jump-rope rhymes, presenting a rich, culturally diverse body of oral literature for storytellers to draw upon. The library and Internet offer countless tales of every kind and culture, but we'll be dealing here with the most common types of stories. The mini-lessons in the second half of this book address the types of folktales above, as well as musical, circle, trickster, square dance, transformation, magical, monologue, moral, porquoi, jump or scary, cumulative, repeating-line, poetic, superhero, and digital stories.

The cumulative tale is a simple story built on basic patterns and phrases that are repeated. There is not much plot involved, but the rhythmic structure of these tales is very appealing to children. Examples of cumulative tales are "The House That Jack Built" and "There Was an Old Lady Who Swallowed a Fly." Another popular pattern is the circle story, a story that ends the same way it begins. Examples are the Japanese folktale, "The Stonecutter," and the book *If You Give a Mouse a Cookie* by Laura Joffe Numeroff. Story patterns repeat in popular children's media, such as cartoons, movies, TV shows, and video games. Through study and practice of story patterns, children can understand the structure of the old tales and create their own.

The best and most relevant stories are perhaps the ones waiting to be told and written by your students. Many children can readily tell traditional tales, and they enjoy and remember them because of their simple structure and repetition or their relevance to that child's culture. The tales are therapeutic in that they teach children how to find solutions to the problems they face in life.

Children find great comfort in knowing that others have the same feelings and struggles as they do. With a minimum of teacher guidance, children can learn to transform traditional tales into unique stories of their own. The telling of traditional tales provides motivation for reading the many picture-book versions readily available and provides relevant background knowledge and vocabulary. Understanding and discussing the structure, themes, and motifs of these stories is a good foundation for reading and writing stories that are more complex.

The term *narrative* is used interchangeably with the word *story*. Storytelling elements include establishing the who, what, when, where, why, and how of the story. Well-constructed plots have a beginning, a problem, a solution, and an end. Plot development also includes conflict, complication, crisis, and resolution. This linear type of story is most common in Western literature. Beautiful and valuable story patterns from other cultures, however, may not be linear.

After children learn to tell their own stories, they can analyze story patterns used in their favorite books and movies. In fact, film adaptations of classic children's stories have been very popular (for example, *The Chronicles of Narnia*, *Because of Winn-Dixie*, *The Polar Express*, and *Bridge to Terabithia*).

The Value of Storytelling in the Classroom

Storytelling is much less common in classrooms than reading books out loud, but many children prefer oral stories to reading. Reading a story and telling a story are not the same. A story remains fixed on the page, the words read one by one. There is a one-to-one correspondence between speech and print. The language of text is more formal than speech. While the reader may embellish the text with vocal inflection and tone, the creative repertoire for enhancing meaning is limited. Because the reader holds the book in her hands, there is much less body movement and eye contact. A reader may enhance the text with illustrations and pause for discussion and clarification, but the experience of being *read* a story is less active and often less enjoyable than being *told* a story.

In contrast, telling a story often involves improvisation and audience participation. A storyteller is more likely to embellish a story with facial gestures, body movements, props, and audience participation. Storytelling is multi-sensory, stirring the emotions and stimulating the imagination. The content and style of delivery are easily modified to meet the needs of the audience. The same story can be told very differently to a class of bright-eyed, eager four-year-olds from how it is told to a group of academically advanced fifth graders.

The audience in storytelling helps create the story. Storytelling is open, fluid, and sensitive to the moment. The storyteller draws upon his experience and culture in telling the story. Storytelling is intimate and the storyteller is an active participant with the children, while the author of a read story is more distant and cannot respond to the listener as easily as a storyteller.

Storytelling grabs the attention of the listener quickly, with the focus on the unfolding external action. Time is more concentrated in storytelling with much happening in a short time. An event described in print might take several paragraphs to convey, whereas storytelling a sentence, with the aid of gestures, may convey the same meaning. A picture is worth a thousand words, so perhaps a storytelling performance is worth ten thousand words. Storytelling can offer more ideas, provide richer communication, address difficult content, and survey cultures more efficiently than reading aloud.

Storytelling is democratic, inclusive, and requires less specialized skills of its audience than reading print does. Like speech, storytelling is natural for children and more accessible than reading. Almost all children are natural storytellers and come to school ready to tell a story. Storytelling capitalizes on the fact that a child's listening level is usually two or more levels higher than her reading level. A five-year-old may only be successful with a baby book, but the same child can easily understand a more advanced children's classic like *Cinderella* when it's brought to life by a storyteller.

For most children, storytelling is familiar and is a starting point for literacy growth. Storytelling can also strengthen the home and school connection as an active social experience that is shared among family. It creates a community in which children learn about and from one another. Storytelling communicates sophisticated content effectively and aids in the development of cognitive growth across the content areas.

Storytelling stimulates the imagination. It develops and enhances a student's response to literature, including his awareness of story structure and sequence. It also improves concentration and memory, encourages critical-thinking skills, and teaches about other cultures and other times.

Examples of storytelling abound in today's classrooms:
- Pre-k children act out their original stories with drawings about their favorite animal's adventures;
- A class of kindergartners retell Eric Carle's *The Hungry Caterpillar,* with original drawings arranged with narration on PowerPoint;
- Third graders present an intercultural storytelling festival by telling the traditions of their families and other cultures they have researched through interviews and primary sources; and
- Fifth graders present a living museum production for Black History Month in which they dress up and tell the stories of famous Black Americans, such as Langston Hughes, Harriet Tubman, and Louis Armstrong.

Storytelling: The Central Connection to the Literacy Experience

Performance Literacy through Storytelling

Because basic literacy concepts like predicting, sequencing, and retelling are an integral part of storytelling, it serves as a springboard to other literacy-enhancing activities as well:

- **Listening.** Demonstrate comprehension by comparing, discriminating, predicting, sequencing, classifying, and transferring information.
- **Speaking.** Discuss a story's themes, retell favorite tales, or invent stories based on personal experiences.
- **Writing.** Rewrite, summarize, paraphrase, write in a journal, research, create original stories patterned on other stories, or write a poem or play version of a story.
- **Reading.** Participate in a choral reading, reader's theater, story fill-ins, add-on stories, or building a tale from key words.
- **Visual Arts.** Create posters, models, collages, crafts, masks, puppets, mobiles, photos, picture stories, blackboard drawings, or multimedia applications with digital storytelling.
- **Dramatics.** Dramatize, mime, and role-play stories; recite tales from prepared dialogues; retell stories; create new stories.

Content-area lessons in social studies, language arts, math, science, and languages also benefit from the predicting, sequencing, and retelling opportunities storytelling provides. Children who listen to stories are exposed to many new words. They may not know what all the words mean, but hearing or reading a story helps them to understand the meaning of the words through context. Furthermore, storytelling builds vocabulary by helping students decipher unknown word meanings through the setting and surrounding words.

In addition to literacy, storytelling also develops important life skills known as the "5 C's": creativity, communication, community, culture, and critical thinking.

Creativity. When children listen to stories, they use their imaginations to create images of the characters and places described by the words. Imagination is the essence of creativity and higher-order thinking. Storytelling gives students the power to use their imaginations to create original work.

Community. Creativity thrives in the balance between self and others, individuality and community. Storytelling helps students find their way to creativity in a social context by providing experiences as a teller and a listener, a writer and a reader. Storytelling bridges school, home, and community. When children and their families work together telling, reading, and writing stories, they learn about their culture and heritage while bringing school literacy lessons home. Likewise, when parents are invited to school to see their children perform stories, literacy is celebrated publicly and positively. After-school storytelling programs give students further opportunities to explore their interests, connect with community, and form positive relationships with adults and peers.

Communication. Children who would not normally get up in front of a class are much more willing to do so with storytelling. When students are successful telling a story, they will engage in it repeatedly and build confidence. Struggling students are usually afraid to put their thoughts on paper. They are afraid to open up to peers and often become disruptive and engage in avoidance behaviors.

Storytelling creates a safe environment for positive self-expression and interaction. In addition, telling stories immerses children in the sounds and patterns of the language needed for writing. Storytelling encourages social communication with meaningful tasks that stimulate language learning and fluency.

Culture. Storytelling encourages inclusion of all cultures in the classroom, thereby supporting multicultural education. Storytelling is truly student-centered because it encourages students to bring their personal cultural experiences, perspectives, and ideas into the classroom. Storytelling helps second-language learners learn to appreciate and share their first culture and the cultures of others.

Critical thinking. Storytelling promotes the critical-thinking processes of reasoning, making judgments, and solving problems. Narratives show how to face the problems of life—loss, anger, fear, illness, jealousy, greed, poverty, hatred, prejudice, and violence—and use imagination to think through and discuss characters' problems and possible solutions. Judging the performance of a storyteller/writer offers a powerful exercise in critical thinking and self-monitoring that students can apply to their own performances by asking their peers, "What did I do to make this a good storytelling? What could I do to make it even better?"

Fitting Storytelling into the Language Arts Block

Most elementary schools try to allocate between 90 and 120 minutes for daily literacy instruction, which includes segments devoted to independent and guided reading and writing, as well as skills instruction.

Because of storytelling's central role in building literacy skills, it's not difficult to find a time and place for it during the block. These strategies will squeeze more time for storytelling into your hectic school day:

- **Take a ten-minute storytelling break.** You and your students can enjoy telling or reading stories anytime. It's relaxing and relieves classroom tension.
- **Use "dead time" for telling quick tales.** Fill those pockets of transition time, like waiting for lunch or right after a test. (See a collection of concise folktale plots for quick retelling at http://www.storyarts.org/library/nutshell/index.html).
- **Click with digital storytelling.** Play a storytelling video or DVD, or listen to a story on the CD included with this book. Connect with online storytellers. Visit www.storyteller.net to listen to audio clips of various storytellers, or search for storytelling videos on YouTube.com.
- **Begin a lesson with a story instead of a lecture.** Introduce a topic with a first-person account of an event—*I was there at the signing of the Declaration of Independence*—or another story.
- **End a lesson with a story instead of a worksheet.** Consolidate and apply knowledge by retelling content as narrative.
- **Ban the boring book report.** Encourage students to retell a book, try a character sketch, or become the author through storytelling.
- **Write with *voice* for an audience, not just for a rubric.** In writer's workshop, let students tell their stories first and then write them. Act out the final draft through interactive storytelling.

- **Present a public exhibition of knowledge through a living wax museum event.** Breathe life into dead history. For example, don't report on Paul Revere's midnight ride—act it out through a story or story theatre.
- **Start a before- or after-school storytelling club.** Combine opportunities for stories, poetry, songs, and even dance with a Performance Literacy Club (PLC).

Fitting Storytelling into the Content Areas and Upper Grades

In middle school, storytelling doesn't have to be relegated to the language arts or English class. Storytelling can be an incredibly flexible and powerful learning tool across the content areas. The advanced storytelling mini-lessons in Chapter 6 present specific applications in subjects like social studies and science.

Storytelling meets the needs of adolescents because it promotes active, social learning. It provides an engaging alternative to the all-too-pervasive routine of "read the textbook and answer the questions at the end of the chapter." Here are just a few ways students can demonstrate their learning through storytelling:

- **Supplement the textbook with trade books.** Content presented as narrative is easier to understand, provides a richer context, and elicits emotional involvement in the topic. Reading *The Diary of Anne Frank* helps students understand and really feel what living in the doom of the Holocaust was like.
- **Build interpersonal communication skills with monologues.** Let students show and tell what they have learned through performing monologues based on their research of famous scientists and historical figures.
- **Be a content expert.** Students become any animal, person, or even an object that they have studied and then tell their stories of fact through a class question-and-answer session.
- **Teach the storytelling study strategy.** After each lecture, tell a story about the material covered. Students can take turns reviewing the concepts learned, emphasizing why this material is important, and how they will use what they've learned in their everyday lives.
- **Create digital stories.** Students can recount historical events, explain complex concepts, or explore their community with a mixture of computer-based images, text, recorded audio narration, video clips, and music.

Chapter 2

Story Development

Performance literacy is the process of teaching students to perform their stories. It embraces the two components of storytelling: story *development* and story *delivery*. In story development, students develop and hone the skills necessary for writing original stories, poems, and other narrative events using techniques of effective story creation.

Stories can be original or adapted from other works, such as folktales. They can be stories in the conventional sense or any other work that lends itself to written and dramatic representation. No matter the story or performance type, five main components emerge as essential for teaching performance literacy, each augmenting either story development or story delivery:

1) Story creating using story mapping with a visual portrait (development)
2) Oral storytelling/retelling including assessment (delivery)
3) Writing the story (development)
4) Retelling, revising, and rehearsing the story (development and delivery)
5) Performing the story within the school and community, including recording and illustrating (delivery)

The Standards-based Experience-Reflect-Apply Mini-lesson

We advocate using the Experience-Reflect-Apply (ERA) framework for creating storytelling mini-lessons that address both state standards and the ways students learn best.

The ERA format applied to performance literacy looks like this:

- Students **experience** a story (or poem or song) through listening or reading.
- Students **reflect** on a story (map out the story pattern drawing a visual portrait).
- Students **apply**, or demonstrate, their understanding by retelling the story or telling/writing a new story.

The ERA format creates a learning cycle that reinforces and creates continual student learning in a whole-part-whole approach. Furthermore, ERA emphasizes the pleasures and value of reading (the whole) and the key skills (the parts) needed for achieving success in reading, writing, and performing stories.

Storytelling empowers standards-based learning in all subject areas. Every state has standards, and those standards always include speaking, listening, reading, and writing skills. In storytelling, students are listening, reading, writing, and performing stories; therefore, they are meeting standards and improving their literacy simultaneously. Students who work hard in storytelling also develop the motivation that will help them on standardized tests.

Start by finding your own state standards online. A place for storytelling can be found within each of the major strands. There is no magic in the standards themselves. However, you can be creative in the way you apply the standards through storytelling mini-lessons. Evaluating how your students meet the standards is essential in today's era of accountability because student progress, high-stakes testing, and teacher merit pay are tied to your students' measurable achievement. You must be vigilant in carefully documenting your students' learning. A writing rubric and a storytelling performance rubric are provided on pages 16 and 28 to help you determine what areas you need to target or re-teach in your lessons, whether it be working on story mapping, description, delivery, rehearsal/retelling, or a final performance.

Before doing a lesson with storytelling, ask yourself the following questions: What am I trying to teach? What do I want my students to learn? What standards can I address with this lesson?

Teaching and Evaluating Story Development

Follow these steps to get story development off to a great start.

Start by telling children a story. Make it interesting with facial expressions, sound effects, rhythm, intonation, and body movement. Paint a story picture, and children willingly become engaged. They sit transfixed, creating pictures and events in their minds. Be sure to brainstorm afterward about what made the story effective, and record the list for later reference. Students will tell you that sound, expression, and movement made it "interesting and fun, not boring!" For a list of good beginning stories, see page 19.

Brainstorm story ideas. Encourage children to write and tell their own stories by presenting them with subjects that are culturally relevant. For example, familiar animals are a good subject to start with because the class will have some background knowledge. As a class, come up with a list of animals. You can limit the list to animals found locally, in the state, throughout the country, all over the continent, or around the world. These can be grouped into a web or another favorite graphic organizer.

Focus on problems and solutions. Now ask students to choose a few animals from the list and brainstorm different problems and solutions (conflicts/resolutions) that the animals might encounter. Write these on the board in a two-column chart labeled "Problem" and "Solution." Try to write at least two solutions for every problem. Here is an example to model the process:

PROBLEM	SOLUTION
Attacked by a predator	Uses camouflage to hide Gets eaten
Hungry	Migrates to find food Adapts to different foods
Pollution	Becomes extinct Humans stop global warming
Pup gets lost	Finds a different mother Mother finds in forest

➤ **Map.** Students create a story map or visual portrait of the story (VPS).

➤ **Tell and retell.** After understanding the concepts of using sound, expression, and movement, students tell their stories to a partner, using these storytelling skills. In retelling, the listener tells the story back to the original teller, who can now see and hear her own story live. Make sure both students get to tell and listen.

➤ **Write.** Students write out their stories from beginning to end.

➤ **Retell and revise.** Students retell their stories in pairs or small groups, listen, respond, and provide feedback about improving their writing and storytelling.

➤ **Done?** Do students need more work telling? Listening? Writing? Literacy objectives will drive this decision and further work in mastery.

➤ **Next steps—perform and publish.** Students work on story development, performing stories for an audience. Students may do digital storytelling by adding artwork and multimedia. Teacher may record stories.

Here is a more detailed explanation of how the storytelling process works.

(Adapted from Ohler, n.d.)

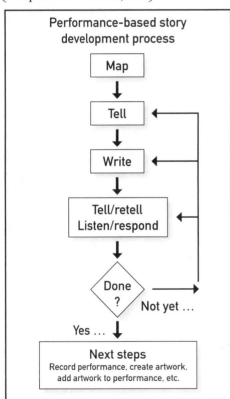

Map. Create the VPS, or story map. After you select a problem-solution set as a class, model the creation of a visual portrait of a story (VPS), also referred to as a story map. The VPS illustrates the concept of an entire story on one page. It is an all-in-one tool providing graphic, text, and sequencing of events. (We suggest using 11" x 17" white cardboard for the VPS.) The VPS is simple, quick to create, and can be a canvas for artists. It provides a snapshot of a story so that the author can use it to tell the most critical parts: the beginning, problem, solution, and end. Students fill in each part as it relates to their stories.

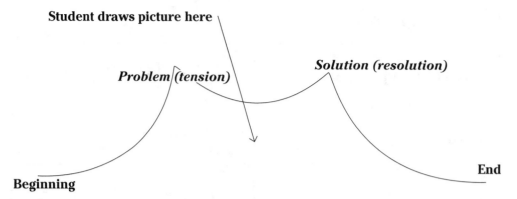

Student draws picture here

Problem (tension)

Solution (resolution)

End

Beginning

Some students find it easier to draw their picture before writing out the beginning, problem, solution, and end. The order of the writing and drawing doesn't matter as long as students can clearly show how their story moves from the beginning, to the problem, to the solution, and to the end.

Problem
The polar bear kept trying to swoop it up with its giant claws. However, the seal kept jumping up through the hole and teasing the bear.

Solution
The bear lets the seal go and tells him to never tease again or he will come and eat him.

Beginning
There was a happy little seal swimming about and a hungry bear came.

End
After the seal apologized, they went their separate ways.

Tell and retell. Once students have mapped their basic story, ask them to tell their stories to each other in pairs. Retelling involves having the listener tell the story back to the original teller, who notes how to improve the story. Students are encouraged to tell and retell before they have written the first draft of their story (the next step of story development) because it helps them create and better understand the story. The combination of oral telling and graphic representation prepares students to *see* the story in their minds and sets up the transition to writing. Students will *tell* words they may not have written down before but are now more likely to add them to their story.

Write. Students are now primed for writing, so encourage them to begin either on the back of their VPS or on a separate sheet of paper. Encourage them to draw a picture that helps them remember the story. Emergent or struggling writers can dictate their stories to a teacher or more competent peer. Encourage children to take risks and to express their ideas as best they can. Talk to them about their drawing, scribbling, and letter forming. Most children respond eagerly to the attention of a teacher who begins "I'm going to write down your story for you as you tell it." As the child dictates a story, write it down on the VPS and repeat the words aloud. Prompt the child if necessary with questions like "What happened next? Is there anything else?" When the child is satisfied with the story, read it aloud together or act it out.

Retell and revise. Next, students practice telling their stories again with peers to see where details are missing from their writing.

Next steps—perform and publish. Finally, students perform their stories for an audience of students, parents, or community members. Students may create and add artwork and publish their stories in print or digitally.

Example: "The Teasing Seal"
Here is a sample story from nine-year-old Abby.
Beginning: There was a happy little seal swimming about and a hungry bear came.
Problem: The polar bear kept trying to swoop it up with its giant claws. However, the seal kept jumping up through the hole and teasing the bear.
Solution: The bear lets the seal go and tells him to never tease again or he will come and eat him.
End: After the seal apologized, they went their separate ways.

One day there was a very happy seal. He loved jumping through holes in the ice. He was having so much fun that he did not pay any attention to the danger lurking nearby. So when a polar bear came running out of nowhere, the seal was surprised. The seal began jumping even higher because he wanted the polar bear to see him so that he could tease him. Right when the polar bear was about to put his nose in the hole the seal jumped out and scared him and the seal said "Ha, ha ha, you can't catch me!"

The polar bear got mad and started to swing his paws really hard but he could not catch the seal. The more the polar bear swung the more he got tired. Then the polar bear gave one last big swing and he caught the seal. The seal was so surprised that he could not say anything.

As the polar bear was dragging the seal away from the ice hole he begged the polar bear not to eat him. "Why should I not eat you?" said the polar bear. "I have a wife and two kids," said the seal. The bear was thinking about what the seal said. It took a while for the bear to realize that family is important, so he let the seal go. Then the bear said, "If I catch you teasing more animals then I will come find you and I will eat you all up." When the polar bear let go of the seal he said "I won't, bye." So they went their separate ways.

Assessment of Abby's Story Development
We think the best assessment of Abby's work is how the audience reacts to her story. However, her story can be more formally assessed by using a writing rubric like the ones provided on the following pages. We caution teachers from being too critical of their students' writing. It is more productive to engage your students in real writing and oral language development than to pick their stories apart in an academic way. Rubrics are simply guides for the teacher to assess students' story development. Use rubrics cautiously and flexibly, because not every writer develops in the same way. Don't use them on every piece of writing- that would take up time they could be writing, storytelling, etc. We have observed a child write a really good story that the teacher criticizes and tries to mold to rigidly fit the rubric. As a result, the child may be hesitant to write at all, and that would defeat the purpose

	BEGINNING/INTERMEDIATE STORY-WRITING RUBRIC
6 **Outstanding**	• The story has a beginning, a problem, a solution, and an ending. • The visual portrait of the story (VPS) is well drawn, creative, detailed, and relates to the text of the story. • There is character dialogue with clearly different voices. • The story has many actions which the teller could act out. • The story has very few spelling, punctuation, and grammar mistakes. • The story has complete, meaningful, and varied sentences. • The story has powerful verbs, descriptive adjectives, and words that create mental pictures.
5 **Very Good**	• The story has a beginning, a problem, a solution, and an ending. • The visual portrait of the story (VPS) is well drawn, creative, detailed, and relates to the text of the story. • There is character dialogue with clearly different voices. • The story has many actions which the teller could act out. • The story has few spelling, punctuation, and grammar mistakes. • The story has complete and meaningful sentences. • The story has precise, vivid, natural language.
4 **Satisfactory**	• The story has a beginning, a problem, a solution, and an ending. • The visual portrait of the story (VPS) is good and relates to the text of the story. • There is some character dialogue. • The story has some actions which the teller could act out. • The story has some spelling, punctuation, and grammar mistakes. • The story has some complete and meaningful sentences. • The story has good word choice with clear meaning.
3 **Fair**	• The story has some good ideas, but they may not be in a logical order with a clear beginning, problem, solution, and ending. • The visual portrait of the story (VPS) is incomplete and does not relate to the text of the story. • The story has few actions which the teller could act out. • The story has limited or no character dialogue. • The story has many spelling, punctuation, and grammar mistakes. • The story has few complete and meaningful sentences. • The story has imprecise words, unclear meaning at times, and clichés.
2 **Weak**	• The story has some ideas, but they are not in any order; critical story parts may be confusing or missing; description is simple and not narrative. • The visual portrait of the story (VPS) is very incomplete and relates poorly to the limited text of the story. • There is no attempt at dialogue. • The story has one or two actions that could be acted out. • The story does not have complete sentences. • The story has many spelling, punctuation, and grammar mistakes. • The story has vague language with few active verbs.
1 **Needs Work**	• The story is clearly not narrative; it is incomplete description or labeling without a sequence of events. • The story has poor word choice and is difficult to understand.

Advanced Story-writing Rubric

	Excellent	Good	Fair	Needs Work
Story Structure	4	3	2	1

The story has a beginning, a problem, a solution, and an end, each developed in distinct paragraphs

	Excellent	Good	Fair	Needs Work
Graphic Organizer	4	3	2	1

The visual portrait of the story (VPS) is well drawn, creative, detailed, and relates to the text of the story.

Literary Pattern	4	3	2	1

The story clearly follows a pattern for a specific genre (folktale, cumulative tale, trickster tale, fable, etc.).

Content	4	3	2	1

The story is engaging and transformative with a moral.

Craft	4	3	2	1

The story uses a variety of literary devices (personification, metaphor, irony, etc.).

Character Development	4	3	2	1

The story has character dialogue with clearly different voices and motives.

Performance Potential	4	3	2	1

The story has many actions which the teller could act out and lends itself to oral interpretation.

	4	3	2	1

The story combines one or more art forms (song, music, dance, or multimedia) for deeper expression.

Grammar	4	3	2	1

The story has very few spelling, punctuation, and grammar mistakes.

	4	3	2	1

The story has complete, meaningful, and varied sentences.

Word Choice	4	3	2	1

The writer uses vivid words and phrases that create pictures in the reader's mind.

What Does Storytelling Development Look Like at the Beginning, Intermediate, and Advanced Levels?

It is the skill development and not the grade level that matters with storytelling. Storytellers can be at any level—beginning, intermediate, or advanced—regardless of what grade they are in.

In **beginning storytelling**, students learn and practice the basics in order to **find their voice**:
- tell stories using sound, expression, and movement;
- brainstorm topics, problems, and solutions;
- create a story map or visual portrait of a story (VPS);
- write a first draft;
- tell and retell to improve stories; and
- rehearse and perform stories for an audience outside of their classroom peers.

A unit on folktales works very well to develop the higher-level storytelling skills that **intermediate storytellers** need to **hone their voice**:
- listen to/read a classic folktale;
- retell the folktale;
- reflect on the folktale's style, content, and patterns;
- map the folktale with a VPS;
- create a new story by using the folktale's pattern but changing story elements (setting, characters, problem, solution); and
- tell, write, and perform the new story.

Advanced storytellers learn how to enhance their storytelling and use it as a powerful community-changing tool when they **share their voice**:
- identify the purposes for telling the story (introspection, entertainment, informing, persuading);
- focus on the audience (age, culture, interests);
- focus on the event (classroom performance, community event/festival);
- choose an appropriate story form (folktale, monologue, jump tale);
- use appropriate literary devices (personification, metaphor, symbol);
- choose an appropriate delivery (traditional, musical, dramatic, digital);
- tell, write, and perform the new story; and
- extend the power and influence of the story by broadening their audience through publication and exhibition.

Grade-level Skills Checklists

The following grade-level checklists can be used to match standards to the stages of storytelling development. Grade-level designations are used only to correlate with the standards, but you know your students best. You should decide when they are ready to advance to the next storytelling stage and in what areas they need more work, no matter the grade level.

Kindergarten

Focus
- Early reading and writing
- Engage children in rich foundational literacy experiences

Sample Storytelling Activities

- Experience many genres of multicultural literature: folktales, myths, and legends
- After listening to a variety of stories, recall details by answering the five Ws: Who? What? When? Where? Why?
- Use wordless picture books for creating/telling stories
- Compare the read-aloud of a book with the storytelling of a book
- Show and tell about something special from home
- Listen to and sing songs which tell stories, then retell through words and pictures
- Draw pictures about an experience and dictate a story about it
- Pantomime a favorite story through actions and movement
- Tell a favorite children's book with puppets
- Interpret characters and the mood of a story through dance
- Experience a wide variety of digital storytelling formats: multimedia, PowerPoint, and e-books

Suggested Storytelling Resources

- *Books, Stories, and Puppets (Ready, Steady, Play)*, Sandy Green
- *Just So Stories*, Rudyard Kipling
- *Sing Me a Story* (CD), Heather Forest
- *Tell It Again!*, Shirley C. Raines and Rebecca Isbell
- The Annotated Brothers Grimm, Maria Tatar, ed.
- *The Random House Children's Treasury: Fairy Tales, Nursery Rhymes & Nonsense Verse*, Alice Mills
- *Across a Surging Sea* (CD), Joy Steiner

First and Second Grades

Focus

- Learning to read and write
- Continue to engage children in rich foundational literacy experiences through read-alouds, storytelling, many visits to the library

Sample Storytelling Activities

- Use key words from stories for developing word walls, word finds, and crossword puzzles
- Focus on new words, puns, rhymes, chants, tongue twisters, figures of speech, and how word choice can enrich a story
- Use a tape recorder to transcribe a story from speech to text
- Use "words in a bag" to stimulate storytelling and word study
- Collect a story about a person from a different culture
- Write and tell a biography about local senior citizens
- Learn a native dance and song to perform about students' family heritage

Suggested Storytelling Resources

- *Give a Listen: Stories of Storytelling in School*, Ann M. Trousdale, Sue Woestehoff, and Mami Schwartz, eds.
- *Keepers of the Earth: Native American Stories and Environmental Activities for Children*, Michael J. Caduto and Joseph Bruchac
- *Out of the Ballpark*, Alex Rodriguez and Frank Morrison

- *The People Could Fly: American Black Folktales*, Virginia Hamilton
- *The Magic Tree House: Books 1-8* (audiobook), Mary Pope Osborne
- "The Hungry Crow" (Hear It! Track #9), Brett Dillingham
- *Three-Minute Stories: Stories from around the World to Tell or Read when Time is Short*, Margaret Read MacDonald

Third Grade

Focus
- Learning to be fluent
- Students develop fluent integration of a variety of reading and writing strategies

Sample Storytelling Activities
- Rewrite a fairytale as a newspaper story
- Tell the story of a famous historical figure students have researched
- Chorally read and perform stories for primary-grade children and parents
- Use rubrics to improve elements of oral reading fluency (e.g., pronunciation, volume, stress, and pause) and performance (e.g., body movement, action, and characterization)
- Identify and record some key features of story language (e.g., the repeating line or the circle story pattern) for students to use in their own telling and writing
- Participate in a school-wide storytelling event
- Listen to a local storyteller talk to the class about delivery techniques: gestures, facial expressions, voice, and props
- Record "follow-along" audio-taped storybooks for younger readers
- Write original stories by imitating patterns of favorite authors: "jump tales," circle stories, legends, and tall tales
- Use basic word processing to write and email stories

Suggested Storytelling Resources
- *How to Write Your Life Story*, Ralph Fletcher
- *Scary Stories to Tell in the Dark*, Alvin Schwartz and Stephen Gammell
- *Sideways Stories from Wayside School*, Louis Sachar
- *Stories Heard Around the Lunchroom*, Jim Flanagan
- *Tapestry of Tales: Stories of Self, Family, and Community Provide Rich Fabric for Learning*, Amy Stuczynski, et al.

Fourth, Fifth, and Sixth Grades

Focus
- Reading to learn
- Build content knowledge
- Develop vocabulary, comprehension strategies, and writing across the content areas

Sample Storytelling Activities
- Research different folklore, and tell legends in a storytelling festival
- Read widely known children's books with social studies and science themes appropriate for storytelling

- Perform and help plan themed storytelling events (e.g., Black History Month, Dr. Seuss's birthday, and Earth Day)
- Conduct author studies (e.g., Langston Hughes, Maya Angelou, and Gary Soto).
- Compare a Native American myth explaining a natural phenomenon like lightning, solar eclipses, or hurricanes with a scientific explanation
- Do digital storytelling about important events and issues within your community
- Model and then ask your students to incorporate sophisticated literary devices (e.g., metaphor, symbolism, and allusion) into their storytelling

Suggested Storytelling Resources
- *Chicken Soup for the Kid's Soul: 101 Stories of Courage, Hope and Laughter*, Jack Canfield, Mark Victor Hansen, Patty Hansen, and Irene Dunlap
- *DigiTales: The Art of Telling Digital Stories*, Bernajean Porter
- *Follow the Drinking Gourd: A Story of the Underground Railroad* (audio), Morgan Freeman (narrator)
- *Joseph Campbell and the Power of Myth* (DVD), Joseph Campbell and Bill Moyers
- *Tradin' Tales With Grandpa: A Kid's Guide for Intergenerational Storytelling*, Vivian Dubrovin
- *Women at the Edge of Discovery: 40 True Science Adventures*, Kendall Haven

Seventh and Eighth Grades

Focus
- Performing stories drawn from historical and literary sources and students' own lives
- Build communications skills with a broad palette: artistic, dramatic, musical, and digital
- Develop critical literacy by exploring identity, tolerance, and social justice

Sample Storytelling Activities
- Tell stories of historical events from multiple viewpoints
- Do creative retellings of favorite books using multiple literacies (writing, illustrating, dancing, dramatizing, singing, and digitizing with multimedia)
- Research, tell, and write stories to explore community, social, and political issues
- Explore identities through storytelling about gender, race, and culture
- Use storytelling for transformation (building community, resolving conflicts, or supporting a cause)
- Challenge familiar stories about controversial people and events by examining what is missing or underrepresented to "tell the rest of the story"

Suggested Storytelling Resources
- *Dare To Dream! 25 Extraordinary Lives*, Sandra McLeod Humphrey
- *We Were There, Too! Young People in U.S. History*, Phillip Hoose
- *Kids with Courage: True Stories about Young People Making a Difference*, Barbara A. Lewis
- *Nobody in Particular: One Woman's Fight to Save the Bay*, Molly Bang
- *The Absolutely True Diary of a Part-Time Indian*, Sherman Alexie
- *Teaching Reading to Black Adolescent Males: Closing the Achievement Gap*, Alfred W. Tatum

Sample Intermediate Storytelling Mini-lesson: Story Development

Now that you understand story development, you can see how it fits into a mini-lesson using the ERA framework to address the standards.

"Sally and the Sea" is an example of a helpful animal tale or animal transformation folktale. The characteristics of such tales are talking animals that impart wisdom and give something beneficial to humans. A person may transform into an animal or vice versa, but the transformation must provide insight into the relationship of humans with animals and the environment. By examining various helpful animal tales, students can learn about living cooperatively with the land, the sea, and their inhabitants. In addition, students can examine and map the story elements of animal tales to better facilitate their reading comprehension and writing proficiency. Finally, students can compare and contrast the fictional transformation of a human to an animal with real-life metamorphosis (e.g., minnow to frog, or larvae to butterfly).

The following reading and language arts standards can be developed with this intermediate lesson on the helpful animal tale:
- Identify themes or topics across a variety of fiction and non-fiction selections
- Record information (e.g., observations, notes, lists, charts, map labels, legends related to a topic)
- Identify the elements of story structure, including setting, plot, character, problem, and resolution, in a variety of fiction
- Compose simple stories, poems, riddles, rhymes, or song lyrics

Experience
Begin by asking, "Do you remember reading a story or watching a movie in which animals provide aid to humans?" (e.g., the movies, *The Shaggy Dog* or *Racing Stripes*). Then, read aloud a helpful animal folktale from the Internet or a book, and print copies for your class. The following stories are readily available on the Web:
- *Antelope Woman*, Michael Lacapa
- *The Fisherman and His Wife*, The Grimm Brothers
- *The Four Dragons* (a Chinese tale)
- *The Little Mermaid*, Hans Christian Andersen

Reflect
1. Discuss the characteristics of helpful animal tales.
2. What are the conditions that cause the transformation from human to animal and vice versa?
3. What are the benefits of the transformation?

Apply
1. Map out the story elements of "Sally and the Sea" using the visual portrait.
2. Practice retelling a helpful animal tale.
3. Write and tell your own original story, poem, or song.

Resources
http://edsitement.neh.gov/view_lesson_plan.asp?id=377
Lesson plans for "Helpful Animals and Compassionate Humans in Folklore"

http://storytelling.whatscookin.com/winners/
Podcast of "The Mermaid"

Sally and the Sea by Brett Dillingham

🔘 **Hear It! Track #8**

Sally Gills was a romantic young woman with eyes that changed colors like the sea—sometimes blue, sometimes gray. She lived in a small fishing village in Southeast Alaska. The land was rugged and enchanting, the weather mostly cloudy, with occasional bursts of sunshine when the sun shone through, or when the winds whisked the rain clouds away.

Sally liked a boy named Irwin, and Irwin liked Sally. Irwin would come up to her as she sat on a rock, looking out over the sea with its waves dancing patterns, the sea gulls blowing about like balsa gliders, great bald eagles sitting like statues in the tops of trees, huge ravens croaking and cawing, their voices hollow and haunting. Irwin would call her name, once, twice, and then Sally would snap out of it.

"Sally, why do you come out in the rain so much? Why do you always stare out at the sea? The village people whisper, they say you are strange. And you are! Why don't you come into the village and watch a movie with me?"

"I'd love to spend some time with you, Irwin, but not watching a movie, not in the village. Let's watch the tide receding, see how the birds wheel in the grey sky, the ripples on the surface of the water! Isn't it lovely?"

Irwin would walk slowly back to the village, sad that Sally didn't come with him, wishing she would be like the rest of the village people and not gaze at the sea all day.

One day, the tide was high and the sea splashed breaking waves with white foam. Sally walked on the slippery rocks, listening for the bark of seals, hoping to see a humpbacked whale fly its 40-ton body out of the water to come crashing down in a monstrous splash, when suddenly she slipped into the cold, turbulent sea.

But for Sally, the sea wasn't cold. It felt just right. And she found she could breathe, just like being on land. Her legs stuck together and formed a tail, her arms turned into flippers, and she swam in the blue waters. Out of the corner of her eye, she saw a fish struggling. It was a huge, silvery fish, caught in a net a fisherman had lost. Sally swam over to it and released it from the plastic lines of the net. At first, the silver salmon barely wriggled, just floated towards the bottom of the sea. Sally waved her flippers and forced fresh water into its gills. The salmon quickly came back to life.

"I owe you my life. My name is Kush-too. You look part land dweller and part fish."

"I guess I am. I'm new to the water. Where is your home?"

"The sea is my home. Come, let me show it to you."

Kush-too showed Sally how to swim with the currents. He taught her how to leap from the water and sail in the air before splashing back to his watery home. They swam in the channels, through huge waves in the open sea, into still tide pools and through the skeletons of dark, haunting shipwrecks.

They swam to a bed of kelp with long, greenish-brown tendrils that swayed gently in the currents. Kush-too danced to its rhythm in the kelp bed. Sally joined him, closing her eyes and letting her body sway back and forth. Nightfall came, and a full moon broke through the clouds, spreading a layer of silver over the entire sea. Together, they swam near its surface, sometimes looking out the water towards land, sometimes looking down into the depths of the sea, until morning came.

"I must go back," Sally said. She swam towards land, her flippers and tail turned into legs and arms, and she walked around the village. She had strands of kelp in her hair. The village people avoided her.

Irwin watched her from his window. She saw him standing there. They stared at each other. Then Irwin turned away into the dark of his room.

Sally looked at the village. The people were not bad—but their life wasn't hers. The movies, the cars, the houses and the clothes...they didn't interest her. She turned and walked towards the sea. When she got to its edge, she kept walking. She disappeared into the water. Kush-too, the lovely silver salmon, was waiting. Her arms and legs turned into flippers. Her whole body was covered with scales. She was no longer a human. Sally was a fish.

On those rare nights when the Southeast Alaskan sky isn't covered with clouds and the moon is giant and silver, beaming its soft light towards Earth, Irwin walks down to the rocks by the edge of the sea. There he sits, staring into the water, until a pair of silver salmon leaps from the still surface, then splashes back. A tear falls from his eye, into the water where Sally has gone.

Then Irwin goes home.

© Dillingham 1999

Chapter 3

Story Delivery

The second component of storytelling is story delivery, during which students focus on performing their narrative events in engaging, creative ways (often with music or visual arts) before students from other classrooms, parents, and the community.

At this point, students will have written their VPS, practiced telling and retelling their story with a peer, and finished writing the story itself. It's now time to work in small groups and get started on story delivery.

Public speaking is an integral and often neglected part of language arts. Storytelling offers an easy way for teachers to develop students' public speaking skills and confidence in front of an audience. The performance skills students learn through storytelling will transfer across the curriculum and beyond.

For students to learn how to perform stories well, the teacher must be a model. You become a storyteller by telling stories. To begin your own storytelling, ask yourself the following questions (Im, Parlakian, & Osborn, 2007):

- What early memories do you have of experiences with books and storytelling?
- What are some of your favorite stories from childhood (books and family stories)? Why are they your favorites? When you recall these stories, how do you feel?
- What are some early stories you heard as a child that have had an effect on you, both personally and professionally?

Teaching and Evaluating Story Delivery

The *how* and *what* of each of the three stages of storytelling—beginning, intermediate, and advanced—are provided within the mini-lessons in the second half of this book. Generally speaking, children move through all of these steps, no matter how old they are. Children do not need to proceed through the stages in lock-step fashion. A good story knows no grade level, so it is fine for a motivated storyteller to work beyond beginning storytelling, especially if the teacher is there to guide him. Similarly, a sophisticated storyteller might want to learn a beginning story to perform for a younger audience.

The following are some general instructional strategies for teaching and improving storytelling performances that should be used at all levels.

Use modeling, feedback, discussion, and guided practice. We have used the following simple but very powerful discussion process effectively to evaluate child and adult storytelling performances at all levels. After the storytelling performance, ask the audience, "What did the storyteller do to make this a good storytelling? What sounds, expressions, and movements did the storyteller do well?" You want students to focus on how the story was told, not the content. Specifically, you want them to think about how well the storyteller used sound, movement, and expression to tell the story. After several students have shared the positives, ask "What could the storyteller do to make the performance even better?" You want the performer to internalize the process so it becomes self-evaluation ("What can I do to make my performance better?").

Model the language of response and criticism. Teachers must model constructive as well as critical feedback without using harsh words in order to teach effective storytelling. Ask "What did I do to make this a good storytelling?" and then model a positive response: "I liked the way you *moved like a fish*, *spoke loudly enough*, *made that train sound*, etc. Follow up with "What could I do to make it even better?" and then model a response like the following: "To make it even better, you might want to *speak up louder*, *pretend to be talking into a phone*, *look scared when the door opens*, etc. Storytellers learn to use variations of these two questions. This language is polite yet direct and useful to the storyteller so he or she can improve the story.

Tell stories in small groups and get feedback. Students tell their stories to a group of three to five of their peers, integrating sound, expression, and movement. Tell the storytelling audience to pay close attention so they can provide feedback about the performance. Upon finishing the story, the storyteller asks the group, "What did I do to make this a good storytelling?" Tell them not to speak out but to raise their hands and wait to be called upon. After two or three responses, the student asks "What could I do to make it even better?" The group responds with the appropriate language modeled by the teacher. In this process, students become open to being critiqued as storytellers (and as writers). Students can retell their stories and target specific techniques from the Storytelling Performance Rubric (page 28) that they wish to improve, such as remembering to use different voices for different characters. After students perform their story again, the group can respond with feedback about how the storytellers improved upon the targeted technique. This type of guided practice increases confidence and improves performance.

What Performances Look Like at the Beginning, Intermediate, and Advanced Levels
As with all new skills, start by teaching the basics and gradually work up to more sophisticated techniques as suggested below.

Beginning
At this level, stories are typically brief, from less than a minute to three minutes. The content tends to focus on personal life, family, and animals. The challenge is getting students to learn the basics: to demonstrate good performer etiquette and speak loudly and clearly.

Good stories for beginners are generally short, have a simple plot, invite audience participation, and can be readily acted out and retold by the children.

Have a beginning storyteller practice introducing herself by announcing her first and last name, saying the story title, and remembering to bow at the end. This instills a feeling of professionalism and confidence in students; parents and other audience members feel respected and know they are watching something special. Another performance behavior you should target at this basic level is voice volume. Have the student practice speaking loud enough so the person at the back of the room can hear. For beginning storytellers, display a poster in the classroom of the targeted techniques. Keep the language simple, and focus on only a few techniques at a time.

Sample Beginning Poster: How to Tell a Story
1. Say your name.
2. Say the story title.
3. Speak loudly.
4. Bow at the end.

Intermediate

At this level, stories are usually longer. They may branch out into areas of the curriculum such as history, science, etc. Folktale plot patterns, themes, and motifs may be integrated. The challenge for children is honing the basics, which require more intense reading, writing, study, and rehearsal. Students' poise, motivation, and confidence are easily affected by peer pressure, so positive feedback is crucial.

Sample Intermediate Poster: How to Tell a Story
1. Be professional.
2. Speak loudly.
3. Use different voices.
4. Tell an engaging story.
5. Show expression.
6. Use appropriate movement.

Advanced

At this level, the stories may range from a short monologue to a longer historical re-enactment. The content not only includes elements of classic folktales but draws broadly from the human drama and the "real stories" found in current events, history, and science. The performance may include more sophisticated techniques such as song, dance, music, and multimedia. Advanced storytellers are ready to research and develop their own standards of performance. The challenge is for teachers to nurture students in finding their own voices and styles and providing the time and place to compose and tell stories. Colleagues are encouraged—and are usually only too happy—to invite your storytellers into their content-area classrooms. The stage enlarges from the classroom to the community. Learning advanced storytelling techniques requires additional support from parents, teachers, and mentors in specialized areas: drama, music, speech, dance, and digital storytelling.

Storyteller's Name _____

Name of Story _____

Storytelling Performance Rubric

	Excellent	**Good**	**Fair**	**Needs Work**
Volume	4	3	2	1

Was the storyteller loud enough to be heard by everyone in the room?

Variety	4	3	2	1

Did the storyteller use variety (e.g., tone, pitch, volume, pauses) in speech?

Voices	4	3	2	1

Did the storyteller use different voices, if possible, for narrator and character(s)?

Effects	4	3	2	1

Did the storyteller use successful sound effects?

Movement	4	3	2	1

Did the storyteller use posture, motions, and performance space confidently and deliberately?

Expression	4	3	2	1

Did the storyteller use facial expressions to convey emotion and meaning?

Professionalism	4	3	2	1

Did the storyteller introduce the name and story title, maintain audience intimacy, and bow?

Performance Tips

The ability to tell a story well is a skill children will develop and hone throughout their lives. The performance tips listed here are for the teacher to guide the students and are generally applicable to all three levels of storytelling: beginning, intermediate, and advanced. Your student storytellers' abilities to integrate all the suggestions well will take time and guided practice. Adapt the suggestions to work well for your classroom, and post the bolded tips in your room for your students to think about and discuss. The performance expectations for a beginning kindergartener are very different than expectations for a more advanced sixth-grade storyteller. See the grade-level checklists on pages 18–21 for specific skill suggestions.

Choose a story you feel passionate about and like to tell. It can be one you have written or one you know from your own experience that you plan to write down later. Telling the story first and then writing the story is easier. You may want to retell a folktale you have heard from other people or a story from a book. If the story speaks deep to your heart, lends itself to sound, movement, and expression, and is appropriate for your audience, you will do an excellent job of telling your story. *Teachers: See the index at the end of this book for suggested literature models to use within each story category.*

Know your audience and choose an age-appropriate story. Make sure the story you choose isn't too babyish or too mature so that you don't lose your audience's interest right away. *Teachers: Younger audiences appreciate highly predictable stories that they can participate in with repeating refrains. (See pages 18–21 for suggested storytelling resources by age). A reluctant child should be encouraged by the teacher to tell a story he created. For kindergarteners and younger and/or shy children, telling a four-sentence story about themselves or their favorite animal is a great way to build confidence.*

Use the visual portrait to review the events of your story and retell it to yourself, a partner, or a small group. Looking at the pictures you drew can help you better remember the events you want to make sure to include. *Teachers: We have found that when children have a visual representation of their story in hand to refer to, it is easy to tell about their pictures and make the story their own. Remember, for young children, telling a story through pictures is easier than through words. The visual portrait is a powerful scaffold for stimulating talk and promoting oral expression.*

Simplify the story. When retelling a story that you have read, it is not necessary to tell it word for word. Learn how to take a flabby, rambling, twenty-minute story down to a lean, five-minute spellbinder.

Warm up and do not let stage fright freeze you. Now that you have prepared your story, you are ready to shake out the "willies." Turn that tension you are feeling into incredible energy to focus on telling your story. Stretch out and take deep breaths, just like before exercising. Warm up your voice by saying silly sentences or singing. Go out, mingle with the audience, and make conversation. You will be less afraid of people you know and with whom you have enjoyed conversation.

Be professional. Enter the performance space with a confident stance. Acknowledge the audience by smiling and making eye contact with the audience. Wait until you have their full attention. Introduce yourself, and give the story title and author. Sometimes you may want to withhold saying the title and author until the end for dramatic effect.

Make sure your audience can see you and hear you. Work as close as possible to the audience. The sound of your voice is your most important tool.

Use variety in your speech. For example, make your pitch higher to show excitement. Use a long pause to build suspense. Make the tone of your voice deeper to sound like an older or larger person.

Use different voices for different characters. A donkey might have a deep, slow voice. A rabbit might have a fast, high-pitched voice. The narrator should have yet another voice.

Use expression. Do not speak in a monotone. The more familiar you are with the story, the more fluent you sound. Tell the story as naturally as a conversation with a good friend, not labored like when you read something unfamiliar. Try showing an emotion on your face before it comes out of your mouth. For example, open your mouth and eyes wide to show surprise.

Use deliberate movements and fill your space. Do not distract your audience with nervous mannerisms such as rocking back and forth, playing with your hair, or leaning against a wall. Do not be glued to one spot. Move in relation to your audience for a desired effect, such as leaning in to scare during a ghost story. Your hands are your best friends in storytelling, so do not put them in your pockets—use them!

End your story as a professional. Remember to bow. Exit the performance space quietly and return to your chair.

Celebrate your performance, and learn from your mistakes. Learn to improve your performance from the audience and teacher's feedback. Do not be disappointed. Learning and growing requires risk. You are closer to hearing applause from a delighted audience than you were before you performed the story. Watch a videotape of your performance and use the rubrics to self-evaluate and learn to tell your story even better. When you feel confident about your storytelling performance, you will want to share it with an invited audience of parents, students, and community.

Games to Improve Sound, Expression, and Movement

These are games you can do with your students to hone their effective use of sound, expression, and movement within their performances. All students benefit from these games, especially those with limited oral presentation and dramatic movement experience.

1) The Expression Game

- Teacher models by sitting in a chair in front of class.
- Student helper stands behind teacher with shield to cover teacher's face (use a file folder).
- Teacher explains to class that they have to be prepared to provide an expression for the teacher to have on her face when the student helper uncovers it by moving the shield. The teacher asks class for examples of expressions (happy, sad, angry, puzzled, sleepy, etc.).
- Student helper covers teacher's face, tells class "Ms. _____'s expression is…," then calls on a student. Student responds with an expression. Student helper lifts shield from teacher's face. Teacher has suggested expression. Student helper then covers face back up.
- Teacher, having modeled the activity, then takes over as the one shielding and game continues.

2) The Sound Game

- Teacher explains that in this game, students must identify what the sound being made is—animal, natural (wind, water, etc.), or machine (motorcycle, door, etc.).
- Teacher makes sound (no body movement), and students guess what the sound is. Pick something fairly predictable, like a rooster crowing or the wind blowing.
- Teacher selects a student make the next sound.

3) Red Rover

- Move chairs out of the way so you have a big space.
- Students line up on one side of the room, all facing teacher.
- Teacher asks a student to decide what kind of animal or person the teacher has to be but does not tell teacher.
- Student recites "Red Rover, Red Rover, please send the _____ over!" The teacher must act out the animal suggested, using sound, expression, and movement while going to the other side of the room.
- From the other side of the room, teacher now leads the game.
- Students who are done get to watch from the other side of the room until exercise is over.

Sample Storytelling Mini-lesson: Story Delivery

The following mini-lesson works for all storytelling stages and is a great ice-breaker. It helps introduce the importance of using sound, movement, and expression in storytelling, as well as how to critique performances. Use the storytelling performance rubric and storytelling audience rubric that follow the mini-lesson to show how specific feedback helps storytellers improve their delivery.

Grades: K–6

Focus: Using sound, movement, and expression for optimizing performance

This is a great icebreaker to get kids interested in telling stories and to teach the use of sound, movement, and expression. We often begin a storytelling show with this story because it is so much fun. Invite an audience member on stage to help you while you narrate the story. Consider picking the most difficult student—the kid who is always in trouble and the one who is always goofing off. Teach that child his part in the story prior to the performance—it only takes about a minute to ask him to listen and go along with the story. Ask him to "disappear" at the very end, hiding behind something so the audience can no longer seem him. If the audience of other students sees their "goof-off" peer having a blast with storytelling, they'll realize that they will, too.

The audience immediately experiences fun with storytelling from the very first story, setting the tone for performances and demonstrating how sound, movement, and expression propel storytelling. This is performance literacy—something very different from the typical, often scripted lesson. It shows how the creative energies of disruptive, disempowered students can be harnessed. We have had success with this story hundreds of times with everyone, from four-year-olds to graduate students.

Experience
1. Teacher performs story with a student.
2. Discuss as a class the role of sound, movement, and expression in performing a story.
3. Read the story silently and then teacher repeats aloud.
4. Students retell the story in pairs.
5. Other students retell the story in front of the class.

Reflect
1. Discuss "the actor from the audience" technique of storytelling, that is, when the storyteller uses the audience to help act out the story. For example, in the performance of *The Three Little Pigs,* the teller asks three children to be the pigs.
2. Why do so many comedians, magicians, and street performers use this technique?
3. Does every story need to be acted out?
4. What other ways might be used in telling the story?

Apply
1. Have students critique each other's performances using the rubric on page 28 and discussing what the storyteller did well and what can be done even better.
2. To do focused work on developing expression, have children take turns using sound, movement, and expression while reading and acting out the boldfaced story phrases (e.g., *transformed into a genie, found a dead fish*). Try making this a pantomime game. Take turns acting out a phrase and see if children can guess the action. Critique each other's expressiveness.

Be Careful What You Wish For...

By Brett Dillingham

Once upon a time, there were two best friends.

They did everything together. Sometimes they would **ride** their bikes fast and **jump** them over curbs and bumps. When one of them would **crash**, the other would say, "Hey, are you okay? Here, use this band-aid!" They took good care of each other.

Or, if they both went to the movies, one of them had a big carton of popcorn and his friend did not have any, the one with the popcorn would say, "Here, take the rest. I've had enough!" They were good at sharing.

Or, if it was a hot, sunny summer day and they were thirsty, one might say to the other: "Hey, let's go to the corner store. I'll buy you a soda!" And they would **walk** to the store.

"Two sodas, please, one for my friend and one for me. Oops, I forgot my money!"

His friend would say, "That's okay, I have some money and I'll pay!" And then they would **drink** their cold drinks.

One day, they decided to take a **walk on the beach**.

One of them **found a squished bug**. He picked it up and threw it at some girls. **"Eeeeeek!" the girls cried**. It wasn't very nice of the boys. But it's what they did.

Then one of them **found a dead fish**. He picked it up by its tail and threw it into the ocean. **He smelled his hand. "Oooh, stinky!" he yelled.** Then he put his stinky hand under the noses of some kids. "Yuck!" they cried. It wasn't very nice of them, but it's what they did.

Then one of them saw something sticking out of the sand. It was an old, brass lamp, dirty and dull. He rubbed it on his t-shirt to clean it off.

Tips for Telling

Enter the performance space and stand at attention side by side. After a long pause, the narrator gazes about intently and states the title as if it were a great secret truth.

Give each other an enthusiastic high five.

Each raise arms and gesture riding bicycles. As narrator says "Jump," both pretend to jump a curb. The friend yells "Whoa!" as he falls to the floor. Gesture to show giving band-aid and pat friend on back as he stands back up.

One performer uses both hands to give a large tub of imaginary popcorn to the friend who gestures eating and making loud crunching sounds.

Wave hand over face as if hot. Both gesture walking.

Narrator says this as if talking to the store clerk.

Friend gestures taking money from pocket and handing to cashier. As narrator says "...would drink their cold drinks," both raise hand to mouth as if to drink and make loud gulping sounds.

Both make big smiles and move arms and legs enthusiastically while walking in place.

Friend walks to audience, looks at floor, bends over, picks up bug, and holds it up high between thumb and index finger as if to study it. Then narrator says "...threw it at some girls" and pretends to throw it at some girls in audience.

Narrator walks to audience, looks at floor, picks up fish, holds by tail high in the air, holds nose with other hand, then gestures throwing. Then as you say "put his stinky hand under the noses of some kids," hold out stinky fingers at students while also holding nose.

The friend walks toward the audience, studies the floor, picks up the lamp, studies it, and rubs on shirt. When narrator says "...smoke began to come out,"

Suddenly, smoke began to come out of the lamp's spout. **It swirled in the air and transformed into a genie**, floating in the sky. Where his feet should be his legs were smoke, still in the old brass lamp.

The genie said, "I am the genie of the lamp. I have been imprisoned for over a thousand years. Because you set me free, you get one free wish."

The boy holding the lamp asked "I get a wish, Mr. Genie?"

"Yes, you get one wish," the genie replied.

"Wait a minute!" the other boy **yelled**. "How come you get the wish?"

"Because I found the lamp and the genie said I get the wish."

"But I want the wish!"

"No," said his friend, still holding the lamp. "I get the wish!"

The **two friends started fighting** over the lamp. They tugged and pulled, each one crying out "I get the wish! No, I get the wish!" The boy who first found the lamp said "I wish you would just disappear!"

Poof! His friend disappeared.

And the genie? **The genie just flew away.**

And the boy never saw his friend again.

He was very sad.

So...

Be careful...

What you wish for...

© Dillingham 2003

friend holds lamp in palm of one hand in front of him as he motions smoke with other hand by moving fingers up and down from palm to ceiling.

Narrator holds arms folded in front of body and sways back and forth. As narrator speaks, the genie floats in the air like a balloon on a string, and narrator changes voice to very low with an exotic accent.

After narrator says the line, the friend repeats "I get a wish, Mr. Genie?" rubbing hands together as if anticipating a great reward.

Narrator must stay in character and use the genie stance and voice when speaking.

One performer says the line as the other repeats gesturing hands in the air in disbelief and irritation.

One performer points at himself with thumb and speaks with authority.

One performer says the lines and the friend repeats with increasing anger.

Both begin fighting over the imaginary lamp as if both were holding onto it. One performer says lines in anger. When performer delivers the punch line, "I wish you would disappear!" he should look irritated at his friend.

Friend runs and hides out of sight. Other performer opens mouth wide to show shock.

Motion hand upward into space.

Pause after line. Look all around.

Show sad face.

After narrator says "So," give a long pause and look out intently at audience. Point directly at someone in audience and say "Be careful....What you wish for" as if giving a dire warning.

Disappearing friend returns from stage. Performers put arms over each other's shoulders. Both bow together. (Reassure a young audience that the friend did not really disappear and that the story is make-believe.)

Audience Etiquette

Teaching students good audience manners requires you to develop, discuss, and model the rules and routines. Prepare your students for guest and peer storytellers far in advance.

To foster respect for storytellers, establish a safe, supportive storytelling environment in your classroom. Remember that storytelling is an intimate, often emotional endeavor with certain risks. Speaking in front of a group is one of the greatest fears in life for many people. Teach your students respect, and do not allow them to laugh at, make fun of, or humiliate any storyteller. Model that storytelling is about supporting each other to be his or her best.

The following rubric offers your students clear expectations for best behavior when listening to a storytelling performance.

Storyteller's Name _____

Name of Story _____

Storytelling Audience Rubric

	Excellent	Good	Fair	Needs Work
Show Respect	4	3	2	1

I showed respect for the storyteller by listening, being quiet, and clapping at the end.

	Excellent	Good	Fair	Needs Work
Be Positive	4	3	2	1

I raised my hand and told the storyteller specific ways in which he/she told the story well.

	Excellent	Good	Fair	Needs Work
Show Support	4	3	2	1

I raised my hand and told the storyteller specific ways in which he/she could make the telling even better.

Performance Assessment and Feedback

After students have written their stories and practiced in front of their class, they can then tell their stories to an audience: their parents, a class next door, a library reading group, patients in a hospital, or anywhere they can "publish" their work. Typically, students rehearse and perform first for their classroom peers, then lower grades (such as fifth graders performing for third graders), and then other classes and places outside the school.

When students know they are publishing their writing for an audience instead of just for the teacher, their motivation increases and they produce higher-quality work. This is equally true of storytelling. Students know their storytelling is good if their peers have told them through applause and positive feedback. This is a powerful and memorable literacy experience, one in which the students' literacy is lived through their own performance.

A more formal storytelling performance rubric and audience rubric can be found on pages 28 and 36.

PART II

The Mini-lessons

Chapter 4

Beginning Storytelling—
Finding Your Voice

Start storytelling off on the right track with these tips for making stories a regular part of the day and encouraging students to find their storytelling voices.

Set an example for storytelling. Getting children to tell stories about themselves and the important people, pets, and events in their lives is fun and easy. Set an example by starting to tell stories, and children will respond with their own stories. Respect your students' voices by paying close attention, being present with them in the moment, and really listening to what they have to say.

Establish a regular time for storytelling. There are many intervals where storytelling can fit, such as during the regular language arts block, before and after lunch, or as extra enrichment in before- and after-school programs. Next, create a simple ritual to signal the start of your class story time. Light a candle, ring a bell, or wave a magical wand to evoke adventures of the imagination.

Find a special place for storytelling. A cozy corner with a rocking chair always works well. One teacher created fireside tales by constructing a mantle and fireplace with cardboard boxes covered in red brick contact paper. A hearth with paper logs and red construction paper flames can add to the effect. Add a candelabra and a Persian rug to your storytelling space and you have a sophisticated atmosphere. Do you need something more portable? Storytelling is flexible and works just as well on the bus or the playground.

Focus on easy-to-tell stories. These stories for beginners are generally short, have a simple plot, are often repetitive, invite audience participation, and can be readily acted out and retold by the children. Start early with your storytelling to establish a routine for the children to write and perform their own stories using the performance literacy process advocated in previous chapters: *experience*, *reflect*, and *apply*. Young children can tell and write their own stories immediately after the teacher models the process. At the start, storytelling needs to be simple with the children recounting their experiences. Have students tell a story about a favorite animal, a trip to grandma's house, or something that they find scary. Expect that their beginning stories will be brief, perhaps three to five sentences long. Keep the stories simple by emphasizing that every story needs a problem and a solution.

Create a visual portrait. This is a great scaffold for remembering and writing a previously told story. Nurture emergent writers by having them dictate their stories as you write them down. Explain that writing is just a talk written down. Have plenty of paper, pencils, and crayons on hand, and encourage any efforts by the children to communicate through symbols, scribbling, drawing, and invented spelling.

Mini-lessons
1. Musical Cumulative Tale: "The Little Red Hen" (Track #1) by Heather Forest
2. Elements of Storytelling: "The Snowy Owl and the Hungry Mouse" by Brett Dillingham
3. Repeat-Repeat-Repeat-Change Pattern: "Four Boreal Owlets" by Joy Steiner
4. Trickster Tale: "The Duck Who Plucked and Plucked" (Track #7) by Brett Dillingham
5. Square Dance Tale: "Barn Dance" (Track #2) by Bill Martin Jr., John Archambault, and David Plummer
6. Poetic Storytelling: "The Sleeping Sea" (Track #14) and "October 31st" (Track #15), both by Karen Alexander

---

Mini-lesson #1: Musical Cumulative Tale

Learning to capture, engage, and enthrall a young audience requires a classic story like "The Little Red Hen," a musical cumulative tale, with its simple plot and catchy refrain that invites participation. Storyteller and balladeer Heather Forest set this tale to music by blending singing with telling. The minstrel style of storytelling uses the rhythm and cadence of music and combines poetry, prose, and song. This style is especially effective for attracting large audiences.

Make your students' storytelling experience musical by letting them add sound effects with a keyboard, shakers, rhythm sticks, cymbals, and kazoos, or simply let them sing along. Check the Internet for sites where children can learn to make and play simple musical instruments. Have fun with sound and *play* music!

Heather Forest suggests considering these key points to start your musical mini-lesson off right:
- Notice the natural rhythmic flow and musicality of speech.
- Make simple, singable melodies.
- Think about why children respond to music in stories.
- Include elements of audience participation in musical tales.

Experience
1. Listen to Heather Forest's "The Little Red Hen" several times. First, listen for enjoyment. Next, listen and follow along by tracking the words with a pointer. Finally, listen to remember the story details.
2. Sing along by joining in on the refrain, "'Not I,' said the animals."
3. Listen to and read other versions of "The Little Red Hen."

Reflect
1. Ask discussion questions:
   a. How would you describe the red hen? The cat? The dog? The mouse?

    b.   What lesson did the animals learn?

    c.   What does the story remind you of in your own life? Have you ever felt like the red hen?

    d.   Why do you think Heather Forest chose to sing the story and not just read it or tell it?

2.   Make a word sort chart of all the rhyming words from the story, and come up with new words to add (ground, found, sound, hound, eat, wheat, beat, seat).

3.   Use a pocket chart to develop fluency. Record and read the sight-word phrases from the story, such as "and the dog said," "and the cat said," and "and the mouse said."

4.   Compare and contrast two different song or book versions of "The Little Red Hen."

Apply

1.   Have the class illustrate the story and post their drawings on the wall. Use the pictures for a group retelling.

2.   Divide the class into teams and have each group perform the story in a different way: choral reading, puppet show, song, or perhaps a PowerPoint presentation with clip art and sound effects.

3.   Compose your own modern-day version of "The Little Red Hen" by keeping the same story pattern but changing the various story elements of setting, characters, problem, and solution.

4.   Retell a familiar story as song. Rewrite the lyrics of a familiar tune and tell a new story. For example, "My Bonnie Lies over the Ocean" can become "My Body Needs Calamine Lotion." Have a class karaoke contest or a sing-along.

5.   Check websites for early childhood educators, such as http://www. hubbardscupboard.org/index.html. This site recommends a retelling of story events by putting words to music. In an adaptation, the children sing a story to the familiar "This is the Way" song. Not only do the children learn to sing a story, they also learn a fun and effective technique for recalling a sequence of events, which is an essential skill of reading comprehension.

Resources

http://www.starfall.com/n/folk-tales/little-red-hen/play.htm?f
E-book version of "The Little Red Hen" in which students can click on the text for an online read-aloud.

http://www.youtube.com/watch?v=JdfvHayuLMo
This video of "The Little Red Hen" features folksinger Malvina Reynolds.

http://www.first-school.ws/activities/fairytales/redhen.htm
A lesson plan and multiple activities are provided for arts and crafts, nutrition, and science in the primary grades.

The Little Red Hen's Song (Traditional)

This is the way I <u>plant the seed</u>, <u>plant the seed</u>, <u>plant the seed</u>.
This is the vay I <u>plant the seed</u>
so early in the morning!

Repeat using the following verses in place of the underlined ones above:

water the wheat
cut the wheat
grind the wheat
mix the flour
bake the cake
eat the cake

The Little Red Hen by Heather Forest
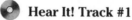 **Hear It! Track #1**

"The Little Red Hen," composed and performed by Heather Forest from *Sing Me a Story.* Recording is used with permission from A Gentle Wind, Box 3103, Albany, NY 12203

Mini-lesson #2: Elements of Storytelling

The Snowy Owl and the Hungry Mouse mini-lesson shows the Performance Literacy Process discussed in Chapter 2, a process in which a student writes a story using a visual portrait (below), then "performs" his writing using sound, movement, and expression.

Student draws graphic using a visual portrait

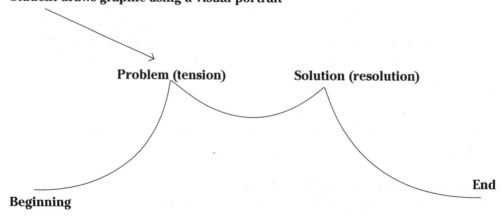

It is important to introduce students to story structure. Students must learn a story's critical parts: beginning, problem, solution, and end. Students should draw a graphic, which is a picture to help them remember their stories for telling. In addition, drawing a personal snapshot of the story provides a scaffold for writing their stories. We find the visual portrait to be useful for beginning storytellers, because it is an excellent tool for developing oral language skills in emerging writers and readers. Those students who are just beginning to understand letter/sound relationships can draw pictures and as many letters or words as they know, then tell their stories.

Experience

1. Tell the story "The Snowy Owl and the Hungry Mouse" using sound, movement, and expression. Begin the lesson by saying, "I am going to show you how to tell and write a story."

2. Draw the visual portrait diagram on the board and say, "Watch me draw a picture that reminds me of the story I just told you." It might be of an owl in a tree, the lynx stalking, etc.

3. Next, discuss the story's critical parts and fill in the visual portrait while asking the students to tell you what happened in the beginning, what the problem and solution were, and what happened at the end:
   - "In the beginning of the story, the owl was in a tree looking for food."
   - "The problem was the owl was hungry, but so was the lynx."
   - "The solution was that the lynx and owl both tried to get the mouse at the same time and missed."
   - "The ending was the mouse got away and got fat eating seeds."

4. Finally, do a think-aloud of how a storyteller and a writer turn a visual portrait of a story with notes into a quick write or first draft of the story.
   - "Now I have a picture of my story with notes. I have the bare bones or skeleton of my story, and I am ready to tell and retell my story to a partner. When I'm done, I will write the whole story down."
   - "After I wrote my first draft of the story, I read it to a friend and we corrected the spelling and fixed the mistakes."
   - "I tell my story with a lot of action. I pretend to be a hungry owl hunting a mouse."

Reflect

1. Have the students do a group retelling of "The Snowy Owl and the Hungry Mouse." Each student tells one thought, such as:
   - Once upon a time, there was a hungry owl.
   - It was winter and he was hungry.
   - He heard a mouse but could not see him.

2. Have students retell the story again in pairs.

3. Have individual students perform the story using sound, movement, and expression.

4. Assess the students by discussing the following questions with the class:
   - "What did they do well in performing their story?"
   - "What could they do to make the telling better?" (See the Storytelling Performance Rubric on page 28.)

5. Have students compare 'The Snowy Owl and the Hungry Mouse" with "The Hungry Crow" (Track #9).

Apply

1. Give the students large white paper (11" x 17"), and tell them, "We are going to write our own animal stories by using the same process. Think of any animal you might tell and write a story about, for example, a hawk, fox, wolf, dog, shark, or turtle."

2. Have students draw and fill in the visual portrait for their stories.

3. Have students tell a story about their animal picture.

4. Do a quick write of the story on the back of your visual portrait. (Emergent writers can dictate their story and the teacher writes it down.)

5. Revise and edit the story with a peer and then the teacher.
6. Perform your story using sound, movement, and expression.
7. Assess story telling and writing using rubrics (see Chapters 2 and 3).
8. Do a performance for peers, parents, and community.

Resources
http://www.youtube.com/watch?v=z_GxhElMQt8
Video: "How to Practice Storytelling Techniques" from Expert Village

http://www.enchantedlearning.com/graphicorganizers/storymap/
Story map graphic organizers

http://www.readwritethink.org/materials/storymap/
Interactive story mapping tool

The Snowy Owl and the Hungry Mouse by Brett Dillingham

The sun was high in the winter sky.

Its rays warmed the green needles of the spruce trees and made the snow bright and glaring white.

The sun began to go down, casting the shadows of the trees longer and longer over the snow. Finally, the sun set beneath the horizon. The only light was from the stars in the sky.

In the tallest tree, a snowy owl blinked her eyes open. She was looking for some food. She couldn't see anything to eat.

Owls can see very well at night, but they also have good hearing. The owl could hear a mouse scrabbling in the grasses beneath the snow. The mouse was looking for some seeds to eat. The owl knew she could not find the mouse under the snow.

Finding no seeds, the mouse began to dig through the snow, climbing up to the surface. The owl heard the mouse's digging.

The mouse climbed up on top of the snow, still looking for seeds. The owl knew she could now hunt the mouse. She leapt from her perch and began flapping her wings towards the sounds of the digging mouse.

The feathers of the snowy owl are so soft they hardly make any noise. The mouse could not hear as the snowy owl came closer.

And closer…

But even the sensitive ears of the owl did not hear the soft footpads of a lynx, which had been hiding behind a tree. The lynx was also hunting the mouse, waiting to pounce when it came near enough.

The lynx saw the snowy owl dropping out of the sky at the mouse, talons open to snatch it up. The lynx asked himself, what would I rather eat, the little mouse or the big owl?

The big owl!

When the snowy owl was just about to grab the mouse, the lynx pounced from the shadows of the tree. The owl saw it just in time and swerved into a snow bank. Only part of her head and one eye were sticking out. She did not move a muscle. Because she was white, the lynx could not see her.

But he was looking for her.

He got closer, and closer, and just when he was almost on top of her, the snowy owl screamed and spread her wings as wide as they would go! She looked huge! The lynx was frightened and ran away.

The owl turned her head around looking for the mouse. The mouse was nowhere to be seen.

So the owl quietly flew back to her tree. She was hungry.

And that would be the end of the story, except for what happened to the mouse. The mouse had run away and hid under the snow at the base of a tree when the lynx jumped out at the snowy owl.

The mouse was shaking with fear. It shook and shook, then realized it smelled something good.

Seeds.

There were hundreds of seeds under the snow at the base of the tree. The mouse ate and ate and ate. It ate so much that its stomach bulged out nice and…

Plump.

© Dillingham 2002

Mini-lesson #3: Repeat-Repeat-Repeat-Change

It is said that the more stories a person knows, the wiser she is. Through a story, we can observe the challenges a character must face and overcome. Stories such as these can encourage and guide our own life path.

Often, story characters meet three challenges and triumph on the fourth event. This story format can be called Repeat-Repeat-Repeat-Change. Students can write their own tales using this pattern.

Read or tell Repeat-Repeat-Repeat-Change stories. Good examples include The Toll-bridge *Troll*, by Patricia Rae Wolff, *Elena's Serenade*, by Campbell Geeslin, and *Aunt Nancy and Old Man Trouble*, by Phyllis Root. Write a collaborative story with the class. Create a story map of the new story. Give students the opportunity to create, tell, and map their own Repeat-Repeat-Repeat-Change story creations.

Experience
1. Create a class story together.
2. Invent a character with a problem to overcome.
3. Think of three challenges for the character which relate to the problem.
4. End the story with a solution to the problem.

Reflect
Create a story map of the class story.

Apply
1. Have students write and tell their own story.
2. Add sound, expression, and movement to the tellable tale.
3. Have students create story maps of their stories.
4. Celebrate the stories!

Resources
http://www.youtube.com/watch?v=_VS9_ZEXjlE
Video of Boreal Owl in Alaska

http://www.birds.cornell.edu/AllAboutBirds/BirdGuide/Boreal_Owl_dtl.html
Boreal owl bird guide

Four Boreal Owlets by Joy Steiner

Once upon a time, in the far far north, in a green green wood, in a tall fir tree… there was a hole. In that hole was a nest with four baby boreal owls.

"Time to wake up," said First. "The sun is going down."
"Move over," complained Second. "You're squishing me."
"Where's dad?" asked Third.
"Mommy!" cried Fourth.

"A-a-ack." Raven landed on a branch close by. "Tok, tok, tok," Raven said. "I see something shiny in that hole. I love shiny things."

"Hoo, hoo," cried First. "Close your eyes. QUICK!"

"That's funny," said Raven. "The shiny things are gone. Oh well. I'll keep looking." Raven flew away.

"Hoo. That was close!" said First.
"Move over," complained Second. "You're too close."

"Where's dad?" asked Third.

"Mommy!" cried Fourth.

Knock. Knock. Knock.

"Hoo. Someone's knocking," said First.

Suddenly, a bird stuck her head into the nest.

"Hoo. It's a sword!" cried First.

"Relax, kids. It's just me, Flicker. That's not a sword. It's my beak. I built this house and I just wanted to know if someone was living here. Nice to see that you have made such a cozy home. So long kids."

"Hoo. She's gone now," said First.

"Move over," complained Second. "It's too tight in here."

"Where's dad?" asked Third.

"Mommy!" cried Fourth.

Suddenly, the tree began to shake.

"Hoo. Someone very big is coming," exclaimed First.

"Hi kids. How're ya doin'?"

"Hoo, Black Bear," complained First. "Your breath really stinks."

"Ho. Ho. Hah. What, fish breath? I just had dinner down by the river. Nice catch. I am headed up to my favorite branch for a nap. Good night kids."

"Huu. Pew!" said First. "Thank goodness he's gone now."

"Move over," complained Second. "I need fresh air."

"Where's dad?" asked Third.

"Mommy!" cried Fourth.

"Oo-o-o-o-o." "Oo-o-o-o-o."

"Hoo!" cried First. "I know that song!"

On silent wings, Momma and Poppa boreal owl flew to the nest. Momma brought a fine fat deer mouse. Poppa brought their favorite, red-backed vole.

"Hoo," said First. "I was really hungry."

"Move over," complained Second. "Snuggle closer."

"There's dad!" said Third.

"Mommy!" cried Fourth.

And now it is time for four little boreal owls to go to sleep. Goodnight.

"Oo-o-o-o-o-o-o."

Sleep tight.

"Oo-o-o-o-o-o-o."

© Joy Steiner 2006

Mini-lesson #4: Trickster Tale

Trickster tales and moral tales intertwine. One difference is that tricksters often get away with, well, with just about anything, even if the trickster is greedy and/or arrogant. Perhaps trickster tales are a way of pointing out to society that life is not always fair. Just as they appreciate jokes, children are often drawn to trickster tales. One of their hallmarks is that they allow for fantastic use of imagination— a crow drinks an entire lake, a raven drops clumps of earth to into an ocean and they become islands.

The Duck that Plucked and Plucked is a variant of the trickster tale—trickster with a twist, so to speak. In many trickster tales the one who is tricked (most trickster tales are animals acting and speaking like humans but with the physical characteristics of animals) is innocent, in some cases greedy or mean. In the tale below, the Eagle is something of a trickster, as is the Duck. However, neither fully takes advantage of the other. They both trick and un-trick their adversary. Trickster, with a dollop of moral thrown in, is included.

Tell a trickster tale with sound, expression, and movement. Draw a visual portrait of it and discuss the problem/solution with your class. Give your class time to read some different trickster tales (some fine web pages below have ample stories). Brainstorm possible tricksters (they do not have to be ravens or coyotes or even living things—they can be inanimate objects!), and scenarios where tricksters could "trick" other animals or people to obtain something they desire. Ask your students to create their own trickster story using examples from the board, or to make one up on their own. Have the students tell and retell their stories in pairs, then perform them for the class.

Experience
1. Familiarize your students with different trickster stories from a classroom book, the library, and Internet sites such as: http://www.americanfolklore.net/ tricksters.html (African American, European and Native American Trickster Tales), and http://members.cox.net/academia/coyote.html (Native American)
2. Invite a parent or local storyteller to tell a trickster tale for your class
3. Invite an older student to come in and tell a trickster tale

Reflect
1. Ask your students if they know anyone who acts like a "trickster," and have them explain why they think this person behaves like one.
2. Outline a few different student stories on the board and discuss the elements that make them trickster tales. Identify the ones that contain morals.

Apply
1. Have your students write and tell their own trickster stories.
2. Have them perform for the youngest classes in the school and for parents.

Resources
http://edsitement.neh.gov/view_lesson_plan.asp?id=237
"Fables and Trickster Tales from around the World" lesson plan

http://www.youtube.com/watch?v=ORuDTRpxEQY
Video of storyteller Joe Hayes and the Gum Chewing Rattler

The Duck Who Plucked and Plucked by Brett Dillingham
🔘 **Hear It! Track #7**

Once upon a time there was a duck.

Quack.

This duck spent the spring and summer on her favorite pond swimming, diving for food off the bottom, enjoying the long days. She loved everything about it except for one thing—

She did not like it when it got too cold.

Then she would fly all the way to Mexico and land in her favorite pond. She would sit there and drink…

Lemonade.

So one summer she was in her favorite pond, swimming, eating food off the bottom, when all of a sudden she realized that it was too…

Cold.

So she started flying to Mexico. But Mexico is far away, and she got tired. She decided to take a nap. She saw a pond and flew down to it. She was just about to take a nap when suddenly—

She saw a shadow on the water.

She looked up to see what made the shadow.

It was an eagle, claws outstretched, about to grab her!

So the duck…ducked!

The eagle hit the surface of the pond. He could not swim easily like the duck—he had to use his wings to row himself to shore.

Meanwhile, the duck who ducked looked up and saw the eagle's feathers. The duck thought, "Quack, I'm going to steal that eagle's tail feathers!"

So she swam up under the eagle, grabbed a tail feather, and—Bink! Plucked it out.

Then she plucked another—Bink!

And another—Bink!

Before long, she had plucked all the eagle's tail feathers.

When the eagle got to shore, he exclaimed, "That duck plucked all my tail feathers! Without my feathers, I cannot fly! If I cannot fly, I cannot get food! If I can't get food, I'll die!"

Just then, the duck who ducked and plucked popped up out of the pond. The eagle said "Hey there, Ducky. Give me back my tail feathers, please?"

The duck said, "Quack quack, not unless you promise not to eat me."

"I promise, Ducky, just give them back."

The duck replied, "Turn around."

The eagle turned around and the duck began putting his tail feathers back. Bink! "Ouch!" Bink! "Ouch!" Bink! "Ouch!" Until the entire eagle's tail feathers were back. Then—

The duck took her nap. When she was rested, she got up and started flying...

All the way to Mexico...

And she is sitting there right now...

Drinking...

Lemonade!

© Dillingham 1998

Mini-lesson #5: Square Dance Tale

This story will introduce students to the telling of a story through music and an American dance style called barn dancing or square dancing. Melody and song carry the story along, according to the award-winning author John Archambault (Stanley, 2006). Archambault stated, "Children and teachers float along on a river of language where music and poetry are intertwined for fluent and joyous language absorption and appreciation." In this lesson, students experience how the poet's three "R's"—Rhyme, Rhythm, and Repetition make for fluent and expressive reading and singing. Additionally, students learn not just how to write a story, but how to compose a story by orchestrating the sounds of language and the expressive movements of dance and artistic images.

 Visit the companion website, http://www.unf.edu/~nstanley/fcat.htm, to read the article, "Interview with John Archambault: Making Words Sing."

Experience

1. Participate in experiences to improve reading fluency through choral readings and performances of the story.
2. View square dancing online at YouTube, or watch live performances or videos.
3. Listen to the "Barn Dance" (Track #2), and have children respond to it through reading and singing along, drawing, or dancing.

Reflect

1. Have children think about and discuss how the author uses rhyme, rhythm, and repetition to tell the story. The student will dictate examples of each as the teacher writes them on a chart:

Rhyme	Rhythm	Repetition
Bright—night	Clap along with the dance	the skinny kid
Leaves—tree		plink, plink

2. Discuss the beginning, middle, and end of the story and have children draw pictures for each part.
3. Compare and contrast reading the story aloud to listening to the story with music. Discuss the differences between telling versus composing a story.

Apply

1. Demonstrate the understanding of square dance vocabulary by having students act out various commands, such as *jump right in, curtsy and bow, swing your partner, now do-se-do,* and *everyone wagon-wheel together.*
2. Play musical pantomime by having children expressively move and dance to musical selections, such as classical, folk, jazz, and rap. As a variation, have students close their eyes. While listening to a poem or story, students use their imagination to draw a picture.
3. Listen to American folksongs, such as "Cornstalk Fiddle," "Farmer in the Dell," and "Old Susanna." Have students retell the songs by composing them as stories with art, movement, and music. Use the Internet to digitize the stories with images and sounds.
4. Choose an animal and compose your own musical tale using the performance literacy process. Change the characters, setting, art, music, and dance to match the child's own context. A barn dance might become a jazz dance with hip cats, a Caribbean salsa with mice, an Indian corn dance with crows, or even something out of the ordinary, like a ballet danced by a kangaroo wearing a pink tutu.
5. After building excitement for composing and performing musical tales, offer books that further explore the intersection of story and song. Try these titles:
   - *My Teacher Rides a Harley.* Gary Dulabaum
   - *Josephine Wants to Dance,* Jackie French and Bruce Whatley
   - *Coyote Sings to the Moon,* Thomas King
   - *Chicka Chicka Boom Boom,* Bill Martin Jr., John Archambault, and Lois Ehlert
   - *Square Dancing (Let's Dance),* Mark Thomas

Resources

http://www.youtube.com/watch?v=vogTVCL-qhc
Video of old time barn dance

http://readwritethink.org/lessons/lesson_view_printer_friendly.asp?id=793
"Improving Fluency through Group Literacy Performance" lesson

http://www.youtube.com/watch?v=ED4aZ3nAnw8
Video of *Chicka Chicka Boom Boom*

Mini-lesson #6: Poetic Storytelling

When teachers interweave storytelling, art, and poetry with rhyme, rhythm, movement, and music, they create wonderfully entertaining literacy lessons which are especially enticing for young learners. Poems can tell stories or just be vivid descriptions, but they are different than prose. Poems are more compact with richer images and rely more on sound and rhythm to convey meaning. The conventions for writing poetry are freer and looser than for writing prose. Many writers practice writing poetry because it improves their prose. We find that music opens the floodgates of children's imagination, creativity, and artistic expression. Teachers who provide children the time and tools for self-expression will be amazed at the results. It can be as simple as the teacher saying, "Close your eyes, listen to this music, and paint what you see." If we would just slow down and put away for awhile the "drill and kill" worksheets, we would see that children can thrive when they become active producers of art. We understand that for some it is a real risk to give kids shakers and drums, let them dance a poem, or have them sing a story. When doing art, be willing to suspend conformity for creativity.

Experience
1. Tell children to close their eyes and imagine what they see as you play the audio tracks of "The Sleeping Sea," (Track #14) and "October 31st" (Track #15). Have everyone share what they saw.
2. Play the poems again as you point to the printed words.
3. Play the poems a third time, but pause the sound as you read the words a line at a time and let the children echo chant.

Reflect
1. Ask the children "What do you notice about the selected poem?" (e.g., It rhymes, has action words, or it paints pictures in your mind.)
2. Ask "What does it remind you of?"
3. Ask "How is a poem different than a story?"
4. Record the children's reading of the poems, and ask them to reflect on their performance.

Apply
1. Let students make their own musical instruments to accompany their reading of the poems.
2. Have students write their own poetic stories about their favorite place or season by composing them with art, movement, and music. Search the Internet for images and sounds with which to digitize the stories.

3. Play instrumental music to inspire the children to paint a picture or write a poem or story. Try the reverse, and let children view art to inspire them to sing a song or dance a story.

Resources

Visit the companion website, http://www.unf.edu/~nstanley/powerpoint.htm, to experience the digital poetic storytelling of Karen's Alexander's "The Sleeping Sea" and "October 31st."

The Sleeping Sea by Karen Alexander
🔘 Hear It! Track #14

The sleeping sea,
Smooth and wide,
Rocks me softly,
Side to side.

Hazy clouds
Shape into sheep.
Side to side,
I drift to sleep.

October 31st by Karen Alexander
🔘 Hear It! Track #15

Ogres and ghosts fly across the night.
Cats dressed in black spring into sight.
Toothless witches waltz across the moon.
Owls atop fence posts hoot WHO? WHO?
Beasts and beauties beat upon doors.
Echoes of "Trick or Treat" soar to a roar.
Rest in peace! Halloween's over!
(And consequently so is **October**!)

Chorus: I hear the beat of the trick or treat feet.

Chapter 5

Intermediate Storytelling— Honing Your Voice

In the previous chapter on beginning storytelling, we emphasized that teachers should:

- Set an example for storytelling.
- Establish a regular time for storytelling.
- Find a special place for storytelling.
- Focus on easy-to-tell stories.
- Create a visual portrait.

It's amazing to watch beginning storytellers—with teacher caring and guidance— find their voices and grow in their poise, confidence, and literacy skills. Folktales are a great way to advance students to the intermediate level and perfect their storytelling skills. Here are some tips to move students to this next stage.

Immerse students in reading, discussing, and retelling folktales. Folk literature represents a substantial portion of the trade books, basal readers, and literature anthologies used for instructing children and young adults. Folktales are short stories that can be read quickly with clear plot lines and easy-to-identify conflicts and resolutions. Retelling folktales improves comprehension. Reading folktales will assist students in communicating in new ways; learning about their culture and other cultures; expressing thoughts, feelings, ideas, and ideals; learning to solve problems; reflecting on their thoughts, feelings, and attitudes; and exploring and discussing the universals of the human condition. Understanding folk literature will improve students' literacy and develop their love of reading.

Study the literary elements of a good story. A good story needs all the literary elements (setting, character, plot, problem, climax, resolution). Students must have a "story sense" in order to summarize a story they have read and to write a well developed story. Additionally, good stories are enhanced with literary devices like motifs, themes, and symbols. Motifs are recurring story structures like "the events of three"—like Goldilocks and the three bears or Aladdin's three wishes. A prominent theme found in folktales is good versus evil. This theme is often represented with symbols such as a sunrise to signal a new beginning and a full moon to signal danger. Literary devices strengthen the meaning and focus of the story. For example, the visual image of a single stone makes the story *Stone Soup* memorable.

Learn and use literary language. Students who experience folktales learn the vocabulary used by writers to discuss stories. Suddenly, they are using the language of literacy—plot, motif, theme, crisis—which will help them tell richer stories, write more proficiently, develop stronger vocabularies, and perform better on standardized tests.

Promote writing with folktales. Folktales provide a great transition from writing about childhood experiences to covering more complex adult issues and topics. They also facilitate the movement from informal oral telling to more formal written narration. The more your students listen and discuss folktales, the more they will blend folktale elements into their own writing. They learn how authors construct texts and how to carefully hone the cadences and rhythms of stories.

The process is quite simple. Do you want students to tell and write richer and more engaging stories? Do you or your students dream of writing screenplays for movies and TV or developing stories for video games? It all begins with a story. Use the mini-lessons in this chapter to show what a folktale is and how it works. With the listed resources, show students how to find more folktales and create their own based on the patterns they see again and again. It's fun for students to transform a folktale into their own personal story. Understanding a tale, truly owning it, is more than just retelling the plot (Forest, 2000). A folktale plot is just a skeleton. The storyteller has to add the flesh and give it life by adding herself.

Storytellers learn to shape a tale in many ways. They can insert a refrain, add special sounds, change the setting, or adapt a story for a different audience. They can shift the emphasis of the story or even the character's motive. It's all about playing with language and literary elements. Imagine a sandbox filled with toy characters: boys, girls, adults, princes and princesses, dragons, rabbits, hummingbirds, trolls, fairies, witches, and wizards. Then add some scenery: houses, a village, a forest, a dinosaur egg, a talking drum, mountains, a sea, anything. What will happen? Will there be comedy? Will there be tragedy? Stories are treasures buried in the sand, waiting to be discovered by storytellers.

Mini-lessons

1. Myths and Poetry: "Blizzard Wizard" (Track #3) and "The UnderToe" (Track #13) by Karen Alexander
2. Transformation Tale: "Raven Day" (Track #5) by Brett Dillingham
3. Magical Tale: "Barcomi and the Flying Dinosaur" (Track #10) by Brett Dillingham
4. Pourquoi Story/Creation Tale: "How Drum Learned to Talk" (Track #12) by Nile Stanley
5. Moral Tale: "Billy and Harry" (Track #6) by Brett Dillingham

---

Mini-lesson #1: Myths and Poetry

Myths are stories about gods and heroes created to interpret natural or unnatural phenomena. For example, in Greek mythology, Zeus was the god of the heavens/sky and controlled thunder, lightning, and rain. Myths are similar to porquoi, or creation, tales. They are powerful, appeal to something deep within us, help explain nature and science, entertain us, and can be springboards for children to write poems and stories.

Experience

1. Tell children to close their eyes and imagine what they see as you play the audio tracks of "Blizzard Wizard" (Track #3) and "The UnderToe"(Track #13). Have everyone share what they saw.
2. Play the tracks again as you point to the printed words (at the end of this lesson).
3. Play the tracks a third time, but pause the sound as you read the words a line at a time and let the children echo chant.

Reflect

1. Ask the children "What do you notice about the selected poem?" (e.g., It rhymes, has action words, it's about nature, or it paints pictures in your mind).
2. Explain how myths and personification in poetry make visible and concrete the ways of nature. Ask how lightning is like the "strike of a blizzard's wand?"
3. Discuss what character traits the Blizzard Wizard and UnderToe have in common. (Both are powerful and could be heroes or villains in a myth.)
4. Record the children's reading of the poems, and ask them to reflect on their performance.

Apply

1. Let students make their own musical instruments to accompany their reading of the poems.
2. Have students work with a partner and write a poem or story to explain snow, wind, riptides, or some other natural phenomenon.
3. Ask students to write their own myth explaining one of the four seasons.
4. Read myths from different cultures, and choose one of your favorites to rewrite from your point of view:
   Greek Myths for Young Children by Heather Amery
   Greek Myths for Young Children (comic-book format) by Marcia Williams
   Multicultural Myths and Legends by Tara McCarthy

Resources

http://www.unf.edu/~nstanley/powerpoint.htm
Visit the companion website to experience the digital poetic storytelling of Karen Alexander's "Blizzard Wizard," "The UnderToe," and "A Sprinkle of Seasons"

http://www.youtube.com/watch?v=3FWq17CT6Cs
Disney's *Fantasia*, the breathtaking, animated film of Igor Stravinsky's "Firebird Suite" (inspired by a Russian folktale about a glowing bird that is both a blessing and a curse)

http://artsedge.kennedy-center.org/content/2231/
Kennedy Center ArtsEdge provides unit and lesson plans on myths

http://www.planetozkids.com/oban/index.html
Planet Ozkids provides integrated resources for teaching animal myths and legends

Blizzard Wizard by Karen Alexander

Hear It! Track #3

When the blizzard wizard strikes
And blows away the leaves
Till all the trees shake naked
And even pumpkins freeze

When the blizzard wizard strikes
And slivers up your sleeves
Till all your fingers stinger
And even nose hairs freeze

When the blizzard wizard strikes
And melts Mister Scarecrow
It's time to huddle cuddle
And THINK SNOW!

The UnderToe by Karen Alexander

Hear It! Track #13

Beware! Beware!
The UnderToe
He hides in the sea
Invisible foe

Beware! Beware!
The UnderToe
He'll spin you around
Like a toy yo-yo

Beware! Beware!
The UnderToe
He'll drag you down
To his home below

Beware! Beware!

Mini-lesson #2: Transformation Tale

Transformation tales, in which people change into animals (and in the case of "Raven Day," back into a human), are found in every culture. Transformation tales represent people's desire to do something impossible, such as flying like a bird or running as fast as a cheetah. But these stories also focus on the risks faced by life forms of all shapes and sizes. For example, the tiny butterfly is threatened by collectors and hungry birds; the majestic and seemingly invincible elephant faces poachers, droughts, and human development; and the water-dwelling salmon is affected by pollution and predators like sharks and bears. Transformation tales show that all life has its struggles.

Encourage your students to choose an animal they would like to "be" for a day, and have them research the everyday life of this animal, including the benefits and risks of being this animal. Or, if you are teaching a specific topic, such as a unit on Australia, you might ask your students to choose an animal that lives in this country. If possible, also provide students with resources, such as videos or the website YouTube, so that they can study the movements and sounds this animal makes. This will allow students to properly imitate their animal, which will greatly enhance the quality of their story, because body movement is a very important part of performing stories. Students will also be much more likely to remember these behavioral "facts" about animals if they perform them themselves, or see them performed by others, than if they simply read about them in an article or on a website.

Story content can be chosen to fit the curriculum. Brainstorm for content focus, then use the Problems/Solutions graphic organizer (p. 13) for students to build their story possibilities. Ask various students to suggest the animal subject(s) and possible problems and solutions. As students provide this information, create a visual portrait of the story (VPS) using their suggestions. Then, ask them to create their own visual portraits, tell and retell their story first to a partner, then tell their story to the class.

Experience
1. Model to the class how to create a story using the desired content with which you have familiarized your students—examples might include the African savannah, the Australian Outback, or animals one can see in the city.
2. Model how to find information on animals in various classroom texts, as well as on the Internet, including YouTube, to see how the animals move and sound.

Reflect
1. Ask different students to model sounds that various animals make.
2. Have your students compare and contrast the problems and solutions from the animal world with problems and solutions that people have.
3. Ask your students to share what they like the most and the least about the animal they chose.

Apply
Have your students tell their stories to a class of younger students and have them share the process they went through to write and perform their own stories.

Resources
http://www.unf.edu/~nstanley/powerpoint.htm
Video of "Raven Day" storytelling performance by Brett Dillingham

http://www.pitt.edu/~dash/folktexts.html
A comprehensive list of folklore and mythology stories

Raven Day by Brett Dillingham

🔘 **Hear It! Track #5**

One day, a boy named Miles was walking down the street, whistling a tune he'd heard on the radio. Miles liked to imitate sounds—elephants trumpeting, roosters crowing, donkeys braying, cars running, jets flying—any kind of sound. Right now he was trying to sound like a flute. Suddenly, he heard a sound like a cat meowing. He looked around, but didn't see a cat. He did see a huge raven sitting in a tree. "Ho there, Mr. Raven, are you trying to imitate a cat?" The raven looked at Miles and let out a loud raven caw.

"I bet I can make that noise too!" said Miles. He tried to imitate the raven's sound, but didn't sound much like it. The raven cawed at him again. Miles tried again. He began to sound more and more like the raven until, finally, he sounded exactly like the raven, because, because...

Miles had changed into a raven.

A raven! My, what a wondrous bird! Black as midnight, almost as big as an eagle, and very intelligent... as well as tricky! He was hungry, so he took a couple of hops and flapped off into the sky. Yes, he was hungry... and tricky.

So tricky that he decided to steal something to eat. He saw a child sitting on a bench in a park, eating an ice cream. Hah, he thought, I'll steal that! When the child put her ice cream down, he flew over and quickly grabbed it in his beak, only to find that all that was left was the wooden stick!

He flew around some more, looking for something to fill his belly. He spied a father and daughter sitting on a picnic bench. The father left his half-eaten sandwich to throw a ball with his daughter. Miles the raven quickly flew over and grabbed the sandwich and began flying off. A huge white ball suddenly came sailing towards his head—the father had thrown his ball at him! Startled, he dropped the sandwich and flew away.

Below he saw a big blue garbage dumpster with the top open. Not being particular about his food, he swooped down to investigate and Yes! The dumpster was full of garbage ravens love, like old French fries and pizza crusts. Just then a gang of crows appeared out of the sky, cawing and flapping, pecking at his tail feathers, making his life miserable. He dropped his food and flew as fast as he could with the crows chasing him, even upside down for a second to defend himself from a particularly aggressive crow, then beat his wings as fast as he could to escape the gang. Phew!

Miles had enough of this town flying. He flew out over the ocean, found a strong air current and sailed up, up and away, as high as the mountains and into the wilderness. He saw another raven and flew with it for awhile, playing in the air, swooping, rolling, and banking together. Then he heard a cry from other ravens... they called, "There is food for all, there is food for all!"

Performance Literacy through Storytelling

He found the other ravens. They had gathered around the body of a dead deer. Some ravens were feeding, others were on the lookout for humans, bears, or eagles. Miles and his new friend fed, then flapped up to a branch of a cedar tree to be on the look-out so others could eat. A family of wolves arrived, but they were no trouble. There was plenty of food for all, so the ravens and wolves fed together. It began to get dark so he headed back to town.

The sun had almost disappeared and long shadows darkened the ground. It had been an exciting day, but now it was time to relax. Miles sat on top of a street lamp and hoped for one last bit of excitement for the day. A boy walked down the street whistling a tune. The melody was so powerful it filled Miles' head with its beauty. He tried to imitate the song of the boy. At first he sounded rough, but eventually his notes sounded just like the boy...

Which he had become. Miles stood on the sidewalk, looking up at the street lamp, where he could barely make out the form of a black raven...

Who was trying to imitate **him**!

© Dillingham 2002

Mini-lesson #3: Magical Tale

The magical tale is referred to as a wonder tale, fairy tale, or fantasy, and is extremely popular with children and adults alike. Fantasy often brings to mind flying dragons, knights in shining armor, and magical spells and can represent an escape from the pressures of life to a fun, magical place. We are willing to suspend disbelief to fly dragons, save a princess, and quest for riches, especially if we are a hero who feels victimized. Barcomi, in the tradition of Cinderella, is one such victim-hero in search of relief from his too ordinary life of slaving away in his uncle's bakery ("Barcomi and the Flying Dinosaur," Track #10). The enduring magical tale still reins supreme, as evidenced by the enormous popularity of such books and films as J. K. Rowling's *Harry Potter*, Christopher Paolini's *Eragon*, and C. S. Lewis's *The Chronicles of Narnia*. Fox Eades (2006) points out that storytelling, especially fantasy, develops emotional intelligence. Through fantasy children learn to express their emotions in positive ways and gain confidence in controlling the things that scare them.

By reflecting upon and analyzing the elements that make up fantasy stories, children develop skills as readers and writers. An important part of children's literacy education is learning the vocabulary used to understand stories. Listed below are the elements of a magical tale readers need to know for comprehension and writers need for composing their own stories.

Elements of the Magical Tale

Beginning	Problem	Solution	End

Where is the story set?
Who are the characters—hero, villain, others?
What is the magic?
What is the problem to overcome?
Does anyone help the hero, and if so, who?
What is the solution to the problem?
Is there a moral or lesson, and if so, what?

Experience

1. Tell or read aloud the story, "Barcomi and the Flying Dinosaur" (Track #10).
2. Do an interactive telling or reading and have students act out the different parts as you read aloud or tell the story.
   Characters: Barcomi, grumpy uncle, Pterodactyl dinosaur, and princess.

Reflect

1. Stimulate discussion on the elements of magical tales by bringing in objects associated with different fantasies (e.g., a magical wand—Harry Potter; beans—Jack and the Beanstalk; dinosaur—Eragon; mirror—Snow White). Ask questions: What makes magical tales different from other stories? What are your favorite fairy tales? Why do people like fantasy so much?
2. Show the Elements of the Magical Tale diagram and ask students to write and discuss the answers to the questions (e.g., Where is the story set?—In a bakery, then in a Pterodactyl's nest, then in the sky and clouds).

Apply

1. Summarize the elements of the Barcomi story with a visual portrait and retell it to the class using sound, movement, and expression.
2. Write your own magical tale or rewrite a familiar one in a comic way (e.g., tell the Barcomi story from the dinosaur's point of view).
3. Do a digital storytelling of your own story. Use the Internet to search for pictures and clip art to accompany a PowerPoint or Movie Maker presentation of the story. Record your performance of the story with sound effects, either as audio or DVD, to share with classmates.

Resources

http://www.youtube.com/watch?v=bpkwhr5P0l4&feature=related
"Saphira" dragon story

http://www.aaronshep.com/stories/classic.html
Aaron Shepard's magical tales for telling

http://www.stonesoup.com/stories?sid=5
Fantasy stories by children from *Stone Soup*

Barcomi and the Flying Dinosaur by Brett Dillingham
🔘 **Hear It! Track #10**

Once upon a time, a boy named Barcomi was walking to work at his grumpy uncle's bakery. It was very early morning and the crickets were still cricking. The birds were just starting to wake up and sing. As Barcomi listened to the birds, he suddenly heard the flapping of huge wings, and a gigantic shadow passed over him. Frightened, he looked into the sky and saw a huge pterodactyl flying away.

Barcomi ran to the bakery. "Uncle!" He yelled. "I just saw a huge flying dinosaur flap its big bony wings over me as I walked to work!"

"Enough of your dreaming!" His Uncle yelled as he brought Barcomi a sack of flour. "You're always dreamin', boy, and that will get you nowhere! You dreamed you saw a dinosaur—so you saw one! No big deal! Why don't you dream you'll bake a thousand pastries today, then maybe we'll get rich!" And with that, Barcomi's Uncle brought more and more sacks of flour for baking, and Barcomi had to work extra hard that day. He went home awfully tired that night and snored like stones as he slept.

The next day when Barcomi woke up, he wondered about the pterodactyl. "Was Uncle right? Did I just dream that ancient bird up? Should I just quit dreaming and work hard to make money? Maybe I should just work my fingers... to their bones!" The thought of his fingers being bones frightened Barcomi a bit, and he thought about it when he walked to work. The more he thought about hands of bone, the more he decided that dreaming wasn't so bad!

Just then he heard the wind as it rushed over the huge leathery wings of the pterodactyl. It screamed a reptile scream at him, "Eeeeeaaaaaawhhhhhhhhhssssssss!" grabbed him in its beak, then flew off!

Now his dreams were too real! Up, up, up he flew in the jaws of the flying reptile, so high that great rivers looked like teeny-tiny creeks, lakes looked like a small spill from a glass of water, and entire forests looked like little patches of grass. He was high! Clouds billowed by like great puffs of white cotton candy. "Where are you taking me?!" he cried at the pterodactyl, but the creature only said "Ughawwwwooooo," because Barcomi was in its beak.

Finally, the beast flew to the top of the tallest mountain in the world. He dropped Barcomi right into his nest. There lay an egg bigger than Barcomi, a beautiful princess, and various jewels the pterodactyl had stolen from all over the world.

"Hey, what's going on?" Barcomi asked.

"I need a good meal for my baby that's about to hatch," said the pterodactyl. "When I flew over you yesterday, you smelled like a sweet pastry, so I figured I'd capture you today and bring you back to my nest. The princess there, she looks mighty good, but I don't know if she'll taste good. Of course, if my baby doesn't want to eat her when it hatches, I'll eat her. I'll eat anything with enough salt on it!" With that, the old dinosaur grinned its huge teeth and flew of into the cotton candy clouds.

"That bone-headed bird sure makes me angry!" The princess spoke for the first time. "The nerve of that point head! I was just dreaming about how it would be so nice not to be a princess any more, you know, all those suitors trying to win your hand in marriage, and me never knowing if they love me or just my money and the fame of being married to a princess! As I dreamed of leaving, that old lizard-skin popped out of the sky like a nightmare, snatched me up in his beak, then flew here and dropped me into this nest. What's your story?"

"Yeah, the big bird-brain did the same to me. I was dreaming about not being a baker when he snatched me up! My grumpy uncle told me dreaming is bad...but I'm not so sure after I see how grumpy he is! At least now I'm not making pastries all day, and I got to see some cool scenery! Hey, I got an idea, let's dream that we can get out of here with all these jewels!"

So they put their round heads together and dreamed and dreamed. Suddenly they heard a sound from the colossal egg. "Hey, dreamers, get me outta here, will ya'?" Barcomi picked up a gold sword with diamonds and rubies and emeralds on the hilt and bonked the egg. It made a huge CRACK and a big, baby, flying dinosaur stepped out.

"Man, it's uncool being cooped up in that egg. It's no fun in there—the yolk was on me!" And with that, the silly bird laughed at his bad joke.

"What's your name?" asked the Princess.

"Baby Dac!" said the dinosaur.

"Are you going to eat us?" asked Barcomi.

"No way, dude! You got me out of the shell, so I owe you a favor! Besides, I don't even want to eat meat—I want to be a vegetarian! Hop on my back, we'll later this nest and see the world!"

Barcomi and the Princess, whose name was Sashita, grabbed a bunch of jewels and jumped on Baby Dac's back. They flew all over the world. Whenever they got hungry, they'd grab pieces of the cloud to eat, because it really was cotton candy, and they stuffed themselves silly. After awhile, they realized they had eaten too much sugar, because their tummies ached and their heads felt like little men with hammers were banging inside. Barcomi asked Baby Dac to fly him to his home, which was right near a river he recognized. Baby Dac's wings flapped, and away they flew.

They landed near the grumpy uncle's bakery. Barcomi didn't want to work there anymore, so he bought it, and then hired his uncle to work for him. He treated him really nicely, and his uncle mellowed out. He was known to say, "Hey, don't work so hard, here, have a pastry!"

Princess Sashita took a few jewels, bought some hippy clothes, and turned into a Flower Child, organizing the Rainbow Festival for the hippies all over the world every year. "It's all so cosmic, isn't it?"

And Baby Dac? He chilled out with Barcomi. He wasn't really a vegetarian, because he ate fish, so much fish that he went fishing every day. Lots of times he'd take Barcomi with him—he'd just hop on Baby Dac's leathery back and flap over to some good fishing hole. There they'd sit, poles in the water, a long stem of grass in their mouths, just dreaming the day away.

© Dillingham 1991

Mini-lesson #4: Pourquoi Story/Creation Tale

"Pourquoi" [por-kwa] means "why" in French. Pourquoi stories are creation tales that explain why or how something is in nature. They have been shared throughout the centuries by many cultures. "How Drum Learned to Talk" (Track #12) inspired by Tejumola Ologboni, or Teju, is an explanation of how the Jembe, a type of African drum, originated. In Africa the drum is used by griots, or storytellers, to perform highly interactive performances of story, song, and dance. *Why Mosquitoes Buzz in People's Ears* by Verna Aardema, *A Promise to the Sun*, by Tololwa M. Mollel, and Rudyard Kipling's tales from *Just So Stories* are popular cross-cultural examples of creation tales.

How did the camel get its hump? Why is the sky blue? Why does the sun set? Where does music and dance come from? Children are naturally curious about all kinds of phenomena, and asking questions is the foundation of learning and the fuel for imaginative writing. Pourquoi stories work well to show children how people from different countries and cultures view and understand things. They are also a good way to compare myths to scientific facts.

Experience
1. Read aloud pourquoi tales.
2. Show pictures or videos of interesting phenomena in nature, such as a solar eclipse, a volcano eruption, a meteor shower, and unusual bird songs, and emphasize to your students the question, "I wonder why?"
3. Read pouquoi tales from different cultures explaining the creation of the world (e.g., Genesis, Native American myths).
4. Watch videos of African dance and music.

Reflect
1. Have students identify key elements of a pourquoi story.
2. Brainstorm phenomena about which students would be interested in asking the questions why and how.
3. Discuss what a World Storytelling Day might look and sound like.

Apply
1. Either individually or in groups write and tell original pourquoi stories.
2. Publish stories with illustrations and embellish with multimedia.
3. Incorporate storytelling techniques and traditions from other cultures into your performance.
4. Contact student storytellers in other countries to learn new storytelling forms and techniques:
   - Africa—drum and dance
   - England—the ballad

- Japan—Kamishiba: picture cards and puppets
- Israel—folk dancing
- Native American—beadwork, weaving, and dances

Resources

http://www.internet-at-work.com/hos_mcgrane/creation/cstorymenu.html
A sixth-grade social studies class project on creation stories and myths

http://www.readwritethink.org/lessons/lesson_view.asp?id=324
Read-Write-Think Pourquoi lesson plans and resources from IRA and NCTE

http://www2.scholastic.com/browse/teach.jsp
Storytelling lesson plans from Scholastic

How Drum Learned to Talk by Nile Stanley
Hear It! Track #12

(Play a drum)
This is the talking drum.
It's for having fun.
Listen to its poems, stories, and songs.

This is the talking drum.
It makes us feel as one. (Play a drum)

But the children asked,
"That is the drum.
But where does it come from?"

The little boy just played his drum. (Play a drum)
Because he liked it, it was fun!
But the children asked,
"That drum, where does it come from?"
He just kept playing his drum.

"Enough, enough STOP THAT DRUM!"
So the little boy said,
"Here is where the drum comes from…

Long ago in West Africa, a little boy was walking in the woods. He came upon a log.
It was hollow because the termites had eaten the insides. He found some goat skin
and put it over the top and tied it on.

The little boy played his drum (Play a drum)
Because he liked it, it was fun.
"Enough, enough stop that drum!"
Shouted a farmer.
"Why don't you take that drum and play it in the fields to keep the birds from
eating my crop."

The little boy played his drum under the sun. He liked it. It was fun. Other boys heard the drum and they made drums, too, and joined in. Soon all the boys in the village were playing the drums. All the girls were curious.

"Where did the boys go?" They followed them to the fields and saw how the birds were scared away by all that drumming. The little birds would fly away quickly but the big birds, like the water egrets, would take off slowly like this. All the girls started imitating the big birds. They liked it. It was fun.

The little boys played the drums. (Play the drums)
It was fun.
The girls danced to the drum
And they all were one.

Boys strung fishing lines across gourds
And strummed along. (Play a guitar and drums)
Everyone danced.
It was a happy song.

But the children asked,
"That is the drum,
But where does it come from?"

The talking drum comes from the sun.
(Play guitar and drums, and everyone dances, imitating their favorite big bird.
Maybe even have a dance contest. All join in with homemade instruments.)

© Stanley 2008

Mini-lesson #5: Moral Tale

The ancient Greek Aesop's fables, the African Anansi-the-Spider tale, the trickster tale of the Raven and Coyote, and the Jack stories of Appalachia (originally from Britain and Ireland) all contain morals, which let the listener know how to behave (and not behave) in a given culture. In fact, throughout history, proper and improper behavior has primarily been passed down from generation to generation through stories. In pre-literate societies, morals and proper behavior are taught mainly through stories passed along orally, through storytelling. Similarly, in literate societies, stories are still the principal way of instructing people on how to relate to one another, only the stories are no longer told exclusively through the medium of oral storytelling. Instead, these stories are presented through multiple media, which include books, newspapers, television, and movies.

Asking children to create their own stories with a moral provides them with ways to understand, in a visceral manner, how their behavior affects other people and, ultimately, themselves. Whether we want our children to learn that it's okay to apologize, as told in the story "Billy and Harry" (following this lesson), to understand the consequences of being thrifty or lazy (e.g., *The Grasshopper and the Ant*), or to teach them about any of the myriad ways we choose to live our lives, the best way for them to understand consequences of behavior is to construct their own scenarios, then tell them to an audience in story format. This forces them to think about the consequences of their actions, identify with others, solve problems, and decide what is right and wrong.

Experience
1. Read aloud several stories containing different morals and ask your students to identify the moral of each story.
2. Ask your students to find examples of moral stories at http://www.timsheppard.co.uk/story/storylinks.html

Reflect
1. Discuss the need for morals in a society with your students and brainstorm as a class morals that are important to the students. Have your students explain which moral or morals are most important to them.
2. Ask students to share real moral situations they have been in.

Apply
Have each student choose a moral and use it to create a visual portrait of a story. Younger students (and some older) might wish to tell their moral tale using animals instead of humans. Remember that since moral tales often contain dialogue, they are a good way to teach a mini-lesson on how to write and punctuate dialogue.

Resources
http://www.aesopfables.com/
Online collection of Aesop's fables

http://www.youtube.com/watch?v=p7vZR5krPHs
Video of Aesop's "The Hare and the Tortoise" from 1947

Billy and Harry by Brett Dillingham

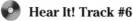 **Hear It! Track #6**

One day, a boy named Billy and his buddy Harry the Hummingbird took a walk in the woods. Ahh, and what a day it was! The sun shone through the canopy of leaves in streaks and columns of light like translucent marble pillars. Insects buzzed buzz buzz bzzz bzzz bzzz, clicked click click click click, zipped through the air, and sang insect songs with their tiny insect instruments. Ahh, the music of the insects!

As they walked, Harry the Hummingbird used his beak to drink nectar from sweet-smelling flowers, whirring around till his tiny tummy bulged as big as a grape—which is big on a little hummingbird! Billy said, "Hey, Harry, don't drink so much or you won't be able to come deep into this forest with me!"

"Yeah, well, I don't think I want to. There are lots of scary monsters and hungry animals when you go deep into this forest, and I don't want to see them!" said Harry.

"What's the matter, are you chicken? Ah-ha, a chicken hummingbird!" Billy said, and he laughed and laughed till he fell, plop! into a bed of leaves. Harry was hurt at being called a chicken, and a tear as sweet as nectar fell down his feathered face.

Billy felt bad about making his friend cry, but he didn't want to show it. You see, lots of people think you're not supposed to cry, and you're not supposed to apologize when you make someone cry, 'cause if you do, they think you're a sissy! And if there was one thing Billy didn't want to be called, that was a sissy! So instead of comforting his good friend, Harry, he left him next to a red rose, tears like sweet soda pop running down Harry's long, feathered face.

"I ain't no sissy!" Billy said to himself, feeling worse and worse about his friend Harry. But instead of going back to him, he started running deeper and deeper into the forest...

The deep, dark part of the forest.

Billy got tired, so he sat on a toadstool. Suddenly, he heard a loud Ribbbbittttt! and a monstrous toad jumped out from behind a tree. "Hey, that's my stool!" yelled the toad. Billy was scared; he didn't know toadstools were really owned by toads! And he'd never seen a toad that big! But he wasn't about to apologize for sitting on that toad's stool, so he yelled, "It's not your stool now, wart-face, it's mine!" The toad blinked his big wet eyes and hung his amphibious head, feeling bad at being yelled at. Billy didn't feel very good about that, and was about to apologize, when he remembered "only sissies apologize, and I ain't no sissy." Billy just walked away.

He walked on alone in the darkening forest. Suddenly the sound of a mournful howl filled the woods. Billy found himself staring at a large wolf standing in the middle of the trail. He was so scared his stomach turned to ice. He picked up a big rock and threw it at the wolf.

The rock hit the wolf. "Awooooooo, that hurt! Why did you hit me with that rock? I was only howling because I was lonely and wanted some friends to talk to!"

Billy felt bad about stoning the wolf, but he knew he should apologize to him but "only sissies apologize, and I ain't no sissy!" So he said, "Get out of here you stinky old wolf, you'll never get friends with breath like that!" The wolf slowly walked away, sadder than ever.

Billy felt bad about making the wolf sad. But he wasn't going to apologize to anyone—not to fat-bellied hummingbird, not to giant toad, not to lonely wolf! Not Billy! Yet deep, deep inside...Billy didn't feel good about himself.

Suddenly, his foot stepped on something squishy, and he heard a loud, "Ouch, you bumbling baboon, you sssstepped on my sssstomach!" A monstrous snake lifted his head off the forest floor. Billy realized he'd just stepped on a huge snake! The snake's head lifted higher and higher, till it was even taller than Billy. He was so frightened his knees shook and his bones rattled!

"Well, don't you have anything to sssssssaaaaayyyy?" the snake hissed angrily at Billy.

Billy thought, "I sure made that big old snake mad by stepping on him, and it was pretty clumsy of me so I should apologize, but, but...only sissies apologize, and I ain't no sissy! So he said, "You shouldn't have been lying there in the middle of the trail, you old inflated hot dog!"

With that the snake began to swirl around in front of Billy's eyes, making him dizzy, and slowly, ever so slowly, he wrapped himself around Billy, then began to squeeze. Billy realized what was happening, that the snake had hypnotized him and was about to eat him, but he couldn't say anything because he couldn't talk, being squeezed so tight and all. He could only think, "Man, what a dummy I've been, thinking I couldn't apologize, that I'd be thought of as a sissy! Now this snake is going to eat me all up and I'll be dead. All because I was afraid to apologize!" And with that, his eyes rolled into the back of his head, and that was the end of Billy...

If this were a different story. But it's not! You see, just when Billy was about to die, his friend Harry the Hummingbird came flying to the rescue, and with his long, thin beak began poking the snake right where his armpits would be if he had arms. The snake started to laugh, and he laughed so hard that he had to let Billy go. Billy quickly caught his breath and he and Harry took off, one running and the other flying through the woods towards home.

When they were almost out of the forest, Billy turned towards his friend Harry. "Boy, do I owe you an apology! First, I hurt your feelings when I didn't mean to and I didn't say I was sorry. Next, you came and saved my life when that huge snake was about to..."

"Billy, Billy, Billy. You're my friend, and friends sometimes have hard times together. I just want to know one thing—did you learn anything?"

"Boy did I ever! I learned it's okay to apologize when you do something wrong! And if you don't apologize, well, you never know when a snake or something else will eat you, and all just 'cause you're afraid of being called a sissy! Anyway, Harry, I apologize!"

"Apology accepted! Let's get out of here before that big old snake comes after us and makes us his dinner!"

And with that, Billy and Harry walked down the trail, listening to the sounds of the insect orchestras playing their tunes, watching leaves twirl in the sunlight, and enjoying the flowers...Billy with his nose, and Harry...why of course, Harry with his beak!

© Dillingham 1991

Performance Literacy through Storytelling

Chapter 6

Advanced Storytelling—Sharing Your Voice

Beginning storytellers can find their story voices with the guidance of caring teachers and performance literacy as the storytellers tell and write their own personal stories. Intermediate storytellers sharpen their skills through learning to integrate the themes, motifs, and language patterns of folktales. Advanced storytellers have heard and told stories of many kinds. They are ready to harness the power of story to define their own identities; share their own ideas and ideals; entertain, inform, and influence larger audiences; and often heal and transform their communities.

Sophisticated storytellers communicate by combining words, images, music, and even dance. Advanced digital storytellers have a variety of tools to magnify and extend their voices to the global stage, including multimedia, the Internet, podcasts, MP3s, and YouTube videos. Skilled storytellers can often find a story to make a point in any given situation. They can turn the seeming chaos of current events into a comprehensible, vivid, and compassionate narrative with a beginning, middle, end and perhaps even a moral tone (Forest, 2000).

The advanced storytelling stage develops an understanding that storytelling is a powerful tool for teaching and learning content, culture, and values. Since ancient times and before recorded human history, stories have educated, inspired, and motivated people. Maxine Greene (1993) stated that the only way to make sense of human experience is through storytelling. We learn by hearing and reading a wide range of human stories. Through hearing many stories, young people may develop the desire to transform society into a place where all voices are heard.

Advanced storytellers may be our future leaders, who have learned to use the power of story to promote active learning in the content areas. Teachers, therefore, should not relegate storytelling just to the language arts. Students will learn and remember the stories of human achievement and events across all subjects. A story holds a listener's attention better than a string of disconnected facts. In social studies, there is the story of how Martin Luther King, Jr. turned his personal dream of ending racial inequality into a generation's dream. In anthropology, there is the story of how Jane Goodall's discovery of tool-making in chimpanzees convinced several scientists to reconsider their definition of being human and spawned a global movement focused on conservation and animal rights. In education, there is the story of Mary Baratta-Lortun, an innovative and courageous elementary teacher, who taught math in some of the roughest neighborhoods in San Francisco, before being tragically murdered. She developed

Math Their Way by combining literature, puppetry, storytelling, and manipulatives to teach mathematics.

Next time you engage children in learning to count with the stories of the *Very Hungry Caterpillar*, by Eric Carle, or *One Fish, Two Fish, Red Fish Blue Fish*, by Dr. Seuss, consider unleashing the power of storytelling in your other subjects as well.

Students need to become literate in the reading and writing of expository materials like math, science, and social studies. Doing well on high-stakes tests requires extensive reading in the content areas. Willingham (2004) summarized the key advantages of storytelling to convey content:
- Everyone loves a good story.
- Stories are easier to comprehend than non-narrative information.
- The structure of stories is more familiar than expository structures.

Mini-lessons
1. Monologue: "Patrick Gas, the Carpenter" (Track #4) by Allan Wolf
2. Magical Animal Tale: "The Singing Geese" by fifth-grade student and "Hummingbird and Elephant" (Track #17) by Brenda Hollingswoth-Marley
3. Exploring Differences: "The Things Willy Wumperbill Saw" (Track #11) by Brett Dillingham
4. Jump Tale: "Pudge Smoot's Golden Arm" by Nile Stanley
5. Repeating Line Story: "I Wouldn't Let It Concern Me If I Were You" by Nile Stanley
6. Superhero Story: "Spudbuster" (Track #16) by Nile Stanley and Ben Brenner

---

Mini-lesson #1: Monologue
A monologue is a form of storytelling by a single person addressed to another person or group. Students can prepare short monologues of their own choosing from books they read or select prepared ones from theatre books or websites. Using monologues is a great way to integrate language arts and social studies. Monologues develop research skills, since in the process of preparing a monologue script, students gather, sort, and synthesize information. This includes taking effective notes to serve as a guide in presentations and for answering questions. Students learn to write with voice, as the monologue requires them to give an eyewitness account of events, using the first person narrative characterized by the use of the pronouns *I* and *we*. The first person narrative allows more immediacy and realism than using the third person narration, which is characterized by the use of the pronouns *he*, *she*, and *they*.

Monologues help students develop poise, confidence, and communication skills as they get a chance to be in the spotlight. Monologues can be honed to become auditions for a part in the school play. The monologues the child tells may eventually mature into adult leadership skills, such as testimony in the courtroom, a sermon in the pulpit, or a call to action on the political platform. Some storytellers become so enamored with their depictions of famous characters that they began to use makeup and costumes and develop a series of monologues into a complete show. For example, actor Hal Holbrook became Mark Twain for many TV viewers.

A monologue does not have to be memorized, and it may be read aloud from cue cards just like your favorite late-night talk show host does. Monologues may be dramatic or comic, informative or entertainment, or a sprinkling of all. Monologues can be composed on the spot extemporaneously or carefully crafted from reading and research. A monologue may be as simple as a comic thirty second account of *my most embarrassing moment*. It could be a poignant, riveting two-minute emotional excerpt from *The Diary of Anne Frank*, which can help students understand and really feel what living in the shadow of the Holocaust was like. It might even be, as in our example here, a story of hope and possibility of an ordinary working person, a carpenter wanting to be an unsung hero who lends a hand in a great epic adventure.

Monologues are a great way to teach to multiple intelligences. Consider using monologues from the following famous people to appeal to your students' learning styles.
- Linguistic intelligence (word-smart): Laura Ingalls Wilder, Abraham Lincoln
- Logical-mathematical intelligence (number-smart): Albert Einstein, Charles Drew
- Spatial intelligence (picture-smart): Picasso, Frank Lloyd Wright
- Bodily-kinesthetic intelligence (body-smart): Michael Jordan, Charlie Chaplin
- Musical intelligence (music-smart): Mozart, Ray Charles
- Interpersonal intelligence (people-smart): Gandhi, Dr. Phil
- Intrapersonal intelligence (self-smart): Anne Frank, Helen Keller
- Naturalistic intelligence (nature-smart): Jane Goodall, Jack Hanna

Through first-person narration, "Patrick Gas, the Carpenter" tells the story of one character's thoughts, emotions, and motives for wanting to join the Lewis and Clark expedition of 1803. This monologue demonstrates the tremendous power that storytelling has to bring to life an epic chapter in our American history. The story of Lewis and Clark has been described as "the greatest camping trip of all time, a voyage of high adventure, an exercise in manifest destiny which carried the American flag overland to the Pacific" (http://www.nps.gov/nr//travel/lewisandclark/intro.htm)

When Lewis and Clark went on their famous expedition to the Pacific Ocean and back they did not venture it alone. More than thirty other people went with them. Each man had his own discoveries to make, and each man had his own stories to tell. "Patrick Gas, the Carpenter" is a verse monologue, in the voice of Patrick Gas, who would eventually become Lewis and Clark's carpenter as well as one of their discovery sergeants. The year was 1803 and the place was Fort Kaskaskia on the Mississippi River. Lewis and Clark arrived in a fifty-five-foot keelboat looking for soldiers to volunteer for the expedition. When his commanding officer refused to let the most valuable carpenter go on the voyage, Patrick Gas approached Lewis and Clark to plead his case.

Experience
1. Listen to the monologue of "Patrick Gas, the Carpenter" (Track # 4).
2. Listen again and follow along with the text.
3. Take turns reading aloud the monologue.
4. Teacher reads aloud examples of third-person narration versus first-person narration.
5. Teacher plays examples of different ways to tell a story from YouTube. Do a search on YouTube or try the following:

    Expedition of Lewis and Clark performed by students:
    http://www.youtube.com/watch?v=1tAQzax-D38
    Expedition of Lewis and Clark by Encyclopedia Britannica:
    http://www.youtube.com/watch?v=oCSzqNfYrIw&feature=related

Reflect
1. Discuss why Patrick "mainly wants to see the trees" on the expedition (every tree is potential wood for his craft, his passion—carpentry).
2. Discuss the definition and characteristics of the monologue. Compare different types such as dramatic and comic.
3. Discuss how first-person narration differs from third-person narration.
4. Brainstorm how to write a monologue: choosing a character, doing research, composing notes, writing a script, making cue cards, and performing.
5. Discuss basic concepts of performing a monologue: script analysis, characterization, props, voice, pacing, movement, and motions.

Apply
1. Practice telling and writing thirty-second extemporaneous personal monologues, such as "my most embarrassing moment," "my many talents," "why racism bothers me," or "why I should be on the crew of the first voyage to Mars."
2. Have students choose a character to base a monologue on. Have them work independently on research, scripts, and cue cards (which should be written on index cards and which serve as prompts when presenting). They should then prepare answers to questions the audience may have about their character.
3. Visit the library and websites to read about and research possible characters for possible storytelling monologues. The teacher might focus and limit the search to a theme (e.g., expeditions that changed the world, Black history, pioneer woman who made a difference).
4. Take a journey through the *Monologues of Multiple Intelligence* reading expedition. In this exercise, the students research famous people to discover their preferred learning styles, and then write a monologue about that person.

Resources
http://www.monologuearchive.com/children.html
Monologue Archive: Monologues from books like Mark Twain's *The Adventures of Huckleberry Finn* and Lewis Carroll's *Alice and Wonderland*

http://monologueblogger.com/
More than 1,000 monologues by searchable categories: male, female, kids, comedy, and drama

http://www.pioneerdrama.com/
Children's theatre play scripts of classic fables, fairytales, and book adaptations

http://www.childdrama.com/
Curriculum, lesson plans, and resources for creative drama

Patrick Gas, the Carpenter by Allan Wolf

 Hear It! Track #4

Welcome to Fort Kaskaskia, sirs.
I know that you have had a rough journey thus far,
and I know that you have plenty of soldiers to see,
so I thank you for taking the time to see me.
Now, Captain Bissell claims he can't spare me
But will all due respect, I'd like to plead my case.

　　Do I have any special skills?

Well, I'm a right handy carpenter.
With the proper tools and a few hands
I can clear you a field of trees in a week
and build you a cabin to boot.
Give me a broadax and a hewing dog
and I'll square the logs if you choose.
Give me a froe
and I'll build you a clapboard roof.
Give me a wedge and a maul
and I'll split a hundred rails in a day.
I can saddle-notch a log
or make a saddle for your horse.
Or a bed for to lie on or a bench for to sit on.
I know the ins and outs of raising a fort,
which I know you'll be needin' up north,
and with your permission, sirs, I've got an idea or two
to expand the capabilities of your keelboat.
I can row and push a setting pole.
I can shoot a gun and throw a hawk.
I can swim like a fish. I can run like a devil.
I'm strong and I'm fit.
I'm a soldier's soldier, sirs.
I never shirk and I do my work.
And I do the other feller's too.

　　What's that? Why do I want to join?

I mainly …Mainly, I want to see the trees.

© 2004

Mini-lesson #2: Magical Animal Tale

Tall tales, such as *The Singing Geese* (written by Jan Wahl and illustrated by Sterling Brown), are found in many cultures, but these tales stand out as an American tradition. Yarn spinners, since before the history of recorded humans, have delighted in telling the most exaggerated stories about animals with extraordinary powers. *The Singing Geese* by Jan Wahl is an African-American version of a tall tale in which a man shoots a singing goose and takes it home to pluck it and roast it. Just as he is about to carve it, the goose raises its head and sings a song, "La lee loo. Come quilla, come quilla. Bang, bang, bang! Quilla bang." A flock of geese that flies through the window answers the song. They lift the cooked goose right out of the pot, they all fly away, and Sam Bombel never goes hunting again.

Illustrated with oil paintings, this tall tale is fun for sharing with children in the primary grades, and the song will have them joining in the singing. Older children can use the story as a springboard to study how authors use literary devices, such as metaphor, allegory, symbols, and personification to reveal deeper meanings. For example, on one level *The Singing Geese* reveals unsettling truths about the slave–master relationship. On another level, it may be a plea for animal rights—a call for a more humane relationship with animals and nature.

Experience

1. View the online video, "The Singing Geese":
   http://stream.unf.edu:8080/ramgen/nstanley/goose.rm
   Fourth-grader Elise Rose retells *The Singing Geese* by Jan Wahl and Sterling Brown (1998). This is an African-American tall tale in which a man shoots a singing goose and takes it home to pluck it and roast it. Just as he is about to carve it, the goose raises its head and sings a song, "La lee loo. Come quilla, come quilla. Bang, bang, bang! Quilla bang."
2. Listen to other magical animal tall tales such as Brenda Hollingsworth-Marley's "Hummingbird and Elephant" (Track #17).

Reflect

1. Recall and summarize the story events.
2. Discuss the stories' use of literary devices, such as personification, metaphor, allegory, symbols, personification, and symbol.
3. Check understanding of literary terms by using a searchable comprehensive reference (dictionary or encyclopedia) with an audio pronunciation guide and pictures. An example is http://www.answers.com/.
4. Compare stories focusing on literary device. Online sources, such as http://www.uleth.ca/edu/currlab/handouts/literarydevices.html, from the University of Lethbridge in Alberta, Canada, provides lists of picture book titles for teaching literary devices.

Apply

1. Write a tale about an animal that has special qualities and powers. The animal can be one that is unusual or imaginary.
2. Retell a familiar tall tale in a new setting, time, and/or place.
3. Try incorporating literary devices into your tall tale to move it from the literal level to the symbolic level for moral, social, religious, or political significance,.
4. Create characters who are *personifications* of abstract ideas that you wish to explore, such as charity, greed, or envy.
5. Have a tall tale storytelling contest and give prizes for the most outrageous, best animal imitation, most entertaining, and best moral.

Resources

http://www.davidholt.com/story/readytales/freedombird.html
The Freedom Bird is a tall tale from Thailand about a taunting melody of a bird that gives us courage because it will not die. Retold by storyteller David Holt.

Doña Flor: A Tall Tale about a Giant Woman with a Great Big Heart (2005) by Pat Mora (author) and Raul Colon (illustrator)

http://www.aaronshep.com/stories/051.html
Aaron Shepard retells magical animal tales from published picture books.

http://edsitement.neh.gov/view_lesson_plan.asp?id=380
National Endowment for the Humanities provides stories, questions, and teaching tips for their lesson, "Folktales and Ecology: Animals and Humans in Cooperation and Conflict."

Mini-lesson #3: Exploring Differences

Accepting and celebrating human differences allows and encourages people to write about their own experiences or their family or culture's uniqueness. Differences can motivate students to create stories. Writing about someone who is different allows students to understand their own strengths and weaknesses and to understand differences in others. Completely fictional, partly true and true "difference" stories encourage students to develop, utilize and expand their imagination and knowledge base to write. When writing about someone who is different, students often write in their own voice, using vocabulary words that may not be part of their normal curriculum, thus adding to their genre of writing styles.

Brainstorm for content focus, then use the Problems/Solutions graphic organizer for students to build their stories. Start by asking the students to use themselves, someone they know, or a pretend person as the subject(s) of the story. Then write these on the board.

The next step, problem/solution, should focus on differences people have that may at first seem negative, but could turn out to be positive. You may wish to provide some examples, such as a blind person, a very small or large person, someone who loves animals, someone who is very poor, or someone who "looks funny." As students provide this information, create a visual portrait of the story using their suggestions.

When the visual portrait is done, model the telling of a combination of subject and problem/solution as a short, draft story to the class. Do not forget to use sound, expression, and movement. Then ask students to choose their own subjects and problem/solution to create their own visual portraits. Pair the students up for telling/retelling. When they are finished, they should fast-write their story. When the fast-writes are completed, students should practice telling their stories in small groups or in front of the class to receive suggestions on how to make their story even better. When you feel they are ready, invite other classes to hear their stories and invite students' parents for a storytelling event!

Experience
Read or listen to "The Things Willy Wumperbill Saw" (Track #11). Model how to create a story in front of the class using real or fictional people who are "different."
- Blind
- Very tiny person
- An animal lover
- Someone who has "eyes in the back of his head"

Reflect
1. Ask a student to tell a true story about someone who is different.
2. Outline the story using a visual portrait on the board.

Apply
Have your students write and tell their own version of a story.

Resources
http://www.youthstorytelling.com/articles.html
Educator Kevin Cordi's comprehensive youth storytelling toolbox

http://www.yesalliance.com/
The Youth, Educators, and Storytellers Alliance offers lesson plans, resources, and links.

http://www.storytellingwithchildren.com/
"The Art of Storytelling with Children" podcast

The Things Willy Wumperbill Saw by Brett Dillingham
Hear It! Track #11

Little Willy Wumperbill was not your ordinary kid. It wasn't the way he looked—he was maybe a little short, a bit skinny, and had a few more freckles than most, but he didn't really stand out in a crowd. No, what made Willy an extraordinary kind of kid was that he always saw things that other people didn't see—things they didn't even think of seeing.

One hot, stuffy day, Willy Wumperbill walked to school as usual. He sat in class watching the other kids and the teacher as the clock tick-tocked, tick-tocked. "Boy!" he thought, "I sure am bored!"

A large, black fly flew by his eye to the window, trying to escape the room. Willy could relate to the fly—he wanted to escape too! Suddenly, he saw a huge polar bear looking into the room. "It must have escaped from the zoo," Willy thought. The giant bear began to climb in through the window. Its head was massive, and Willy could see how hungry it was! The polar bear was about to eat Melanie Whiteshoes (who Willy secretly liked), so Willy got out his trusty straw with a spitball in it and deftly shot the polar bear in the eye. It quickly turned around and jumped out the window.

"Willy!" yelled the teacher, Mr. Boreon. "You know you're not allowed to shoot spitballs in class!" Poor Willy Wumperbill was sent to the principal's office.

When he got to the principal's office, he had to sit in a room all by himself. There was an old rug on the floor. Willy looked at it closely. It wasn't a rug! It was a boat! Willy jumped into the boat and began rowing in the high seas. There was blue sky all around him—except for a few dark clouds on the horizon. As Willy looked, the clouds began rushing towards him real fast! A bolt of lightning shot out of the sky and crashed into the water right next to him—illuminating a huge shark! The shark looked up at Willy with its cold, hungry eye. Shivers went up and down Willy's spine. He looked around for a weapon...nothing! Then he looked at the oars in his hands. Willy broke one so he'd have a sharp point on it. Lightening struck again just as the shark's giant gray head lifted out of the water, jaws open, row upon row of white teeth ready to bite Willy, who stuck the oar in the shark's mouth just as...

The Principal, Ms. Woodhands, opened her office door. "We're sending you home for the day, Willy. You violated school rule X9.4001.007, Spitballs from a Straw. We're sending you home with a note for your parents to sign. By the way, why are you sitting on my rug? You look as if positively frightened!"

Little Willy Wumperbill walked home, feeling a bit dejected by the day's events. Didn't anybody else see what was happening in the world around him? Why was he the only one who saw polar bears? Why was he the only one who saw sharks? Why was he the only one who saw...just then, a large building in front of him began to shimmer. It began to change shape, seemed to grow a tail, a pair of powerful legs, and a monstrous head—it was a dinosaur, a Tyrannosaurus rex! The colossal Tyrannosaur swiveled its massive head from side to side, looking for a fresh morsel to eat. It spied little Willy on the sidewalk. "I must look like a tasty tidbit to that overgrown iguana!" thought Willy. He turned and ran as fast as his short legs could take him. Behind him, he heard the great Tyrannosaurus roar, then felt the ground shudder beneath him as the ferocious dinosaur began to chase him. He ran across a street, turned around, and looked as the huge paws of the monster crushed a car as easily as Willy could crush a toy. Poor Willy ran even faster, but he could feel the earth shake as the hungry Tyrannosaurus got closer, closer. Willy could feel its hot breath on the back of his neck; he knew he was a goner...

A tunnel! Willy saw a tunnel just ahead of him! With his last bit of strength, Willy's tiny legs pumped with all his might, and he ducked into the tunnel just as the dinosaur's jaws tried to snap him up, but instead of eating Willy, his head smacked the roof of the tunnel.

Out of breath, Willy walked further and further into the darkness of the tunnel, barely hearing the roars of the frustrated beast outside. Willy looked around him—why, he wasn't in a tunnel at all! It was a cave! A couple of bats flew near his head, and he almost tripped over a skull, white as vanilla ice cream, staring hollow-eyed at his feet. A huge rat scurried over to him and asked if he'd like a ride to the other end of the cave. Willy was scared of the giant rat, but then he heard the roar of the Tyrannosaurus outside, so he said "Sure." Willy hopped on the rat's back, grabbed a handful of fur and away they went, shooting through the tunnel lickety-split, fast as the fastest race horse, till they got to the other side. Willy dismounted, thanked the kind rat, and walked out into the sunshine.

Willy was almost home when he saw an old man walking down the street. He had long white hair and a beard. As Willy looked closer, he noticed the old man had tiny stars circling around him—he must be a Wizard! Willy looked up in wonder as the old man came near. "Well, what are you looking at, young man?"

"You, you look like a Wizard!"

"Funny you should say that, because I am one! However, very few people realize it... they just don't see who I truly am. As a matter of fact, in order for you to know I'm a Wizard, you must be magic as well! I certainly enjoy it." The wizard produced a rose from thin air and deeply inhaled its sweet perfume. "Here. Give this to your Mother." The Wizard walked down the street, Willy watching every step he took. Then he ran up the porch and went inside his house.

As Willy Wumperbill got older, he saw magic everywhere. He began to be able to control it—he created fewer and fewer monsters and more and more beauty. For instance, when he walked outside and saw the moon, he could jet himself up to it in a matter of minutes, and cruise around its silvery surface. Or if he ate a cupcake at a birthday party, but was still hungry, he could shrink himself to the size of an ant, then stuff himself on crumbs as big as basketballs. Sometimes at night he would transform his little rug into a magic carpet. Then he would open his window and fly all over his neighborhood. Sometimes the skaters would see him gliding over the tops of trees and yell out "There goes Willy, check him out!" and Willy would wave and smile until he disappeared from sight. There were very few things Willy couldn't do.

Little Willy Wumperbill saw things that other people didn't see—and because of it, Willy led a fantastic life.

The End.

© Dillingham 1998

Mini-Lesson #4: Jump Tale

The jump tale is a scary story in which the teller uses the dramatic pause followed by a sudden loud outburst to scare the audience and get them to jump out of their seats. Jump tales usually involve a ghost seeking revenge. Mark Twain's (1897) *Golden Arm* is the classic jump tale with a story pattern children love to copy and retell as their own ghost stories around the campfire, on the playground, or at slumber parties. In the classroom, teachers can capitalize on children's love of scary stories. Jump tales provide opportunities for storytelling with dramatic expression, analyzing story pattern, and writing with voice. Teach children to tell the jump tale using multiple techniques. Tell it solo, as an interactive group, or script and perform as a reader's theater. Do digital storytelling. Use multimedia to add art, music, and sound effects. Make an audio CD or video on the Web or on a DVD.

Experience
1. Tell or read aloud jump tales readily available on the Web and in books:
    - "The Golden Arm" by Mark Twain
      (http://www.folktale.net/golden_arm.html)
    - "Teeny-Tiny" (http://www.sacred-texts.com/neu/eng/eft/eft13.htm)
    - "Dead Man's Liver" (http://www.folktale.net/liver.html)
2. Tell and read the jump tale "Pudge Smoot's Golden Arm" by Nile Stanley.

Reflect
1. Have your class do a teacher guided group retelling of a jump tale. One student begins, "Once upon a time…" The next student adds, "And then…"
2. Outline a chart of the story with the five "W's": who, what, when, where, and why.
3. Compare and contrast using a Venn Diagram, an original jump tale (e.g., Mark Twain's "Golden Arm" with Nile Stanley's "Pudge Smoot's Golden Arm").

Apply
1. Turn the story into script and perform as story theatre. Assign the various speaking parts (e.g., narrator, Pudge Smoot, kids, teacher, and the ghost). Make a DVD of the performance.
2. Write and tell your own version of a jump tale. Keep the basic plot pattern the same, but use your own experience to cast the story in a new place and time. Draw upon the people you know to create new characters.
3. Interview and record a family member's recollections of ghost stories. Transcribe the text of a story into a one page skeleton outline to facilitate retelling. Learn the" bare bones" of a story that give the basic sequence of characters and events.
4. After building excitement for telling and writing jump tales, offer books that further explore the ghost story genre.

Resources
The Dark-Thirty: Southern Tales of the Supernatural by Patricia C. McKissack and Brian Pinkney (illustrator)

More Short & Shivery: Thirty Terrifying Tales by Robert D. San Souci, Katherine Coville (illustrator), and Jacqueline Rogers (illustrator)

Scary Stories: More Tales to Chill Your Bones by Alvin Schwartz and Stephen Gammell (illustrator)

Pudge Smoot's Golden Arm by Nile Stanley

The family had great hopes for their son, Clarence Douglas Farnsworth Smoot, the third. Unfortunately no one could remember a name that long so everybody called the boy, Pudge Smoot. The name fit just fine because he was chubby. Now Pudge was very popular among his classmates because he could throw and hit a baseball better than anybody.

"That Pudge Smoot's got a golden arm," all the kids would say.

"I don't know," Pudge would always say. (Say in an exaggerated tone of stupidity and apology.)

Despite being slow-witted he was always picked first to play baseball in gym class and his team always won.

In class Pudge was a class clown even though he didn't try to be.

"What's the capital of Florida?" the teacher asked.
"I don't know. said Pudge. The kids would chuckle
"What's 2 + 2?, in disbelief the teacher would ask.
"I don't know! said Pudge. The kids would howl.

Years later when Pudge Smoot led his high school baseball team to the state championship people always summed him up by saying, "He ain't too bright but who cares? Pudge Smoot's got a golden arm."

Pudge lived on a farm and because he had grown so big he could do a lot of chores to help out his widowed mom. One day Pudge was helping his mom bale hay. He would rake and pickup fresh cut alfalfa and put it in the baling machine. (Repeat picking up and placing the hay into the machine.)

"Be careful Pudge not to get pinched by the baling machine," mom warned.
"I don't know," said Pudge.
Suddenly Pudge's whole arm got caught and mangled in the machine.At the hospital old doc Smithers said that his arm could not be saved and had to be amputated.

Without an arm Pudge couldn't play baseball very well. (Pull your arm up your sleeve in hide it in your shirt. Make flailing motions with your armless sleeve.) The kids stopped playing with him. Pudge grew even heavier as years went by. (Clasp hands and extend your arms beyond your belly.) He could not get into college so he worked on the farm. Pudge grew very sad as he missed the cheering crowds. His mother felt sorry for him.

One day Pudge heard his mom screaming. "We have won the Florida lottery!" she yelled.
"I don't know? said Pudge.
"You idiot, WE HAVE WON THE LOTTERY! We are rich!"

"I don't know," said Pudge.

"Nevermind, you ..." She caught herself and felt ashamed for almost calling Pudge a bad name.

She came back from town with a long wooden box. Inside was a beautiful golden arm—all solid gold from the shoulder down. A real golden arm that Pudge could wear. (Bring your arm back into your shirt sleeve and show it off.) Now he would be happy and popular again.

People noticed right away and said, "Pudge Smoot's got a golden arm."

"I don't know," was all he could say.

"I'm gonna get me that golden arm," said a bad boy Eddy Johnson who recently had flunked out of college and worked at the Whataburger. Also he had a lifetime of bitter memories of always striking out when Pudge was on the plate.

One night as Pudge slept and snored, Eddy snuck to his window. He climbed in and knocked the sleeping Pudge over the head with a baseball bat lying next to his bed. Eddy took the prize golden arm and hid it under his bed. Like Pudge he slept with an open window. Then he was roused out of a deep sleep by the wind.

"Whoo...Whoo..." (Whisper with a whistle.) "Whooo's...got...myyyy...gooolden aaarm?"

Eddy waked with a start and looked around and listened but heard nothing. "Just some gas from that corn dog I had," he thought and rolled over and went back to sleep.

"Whoo...Whoo..." (Louder with a whistle.) "Whooo's...got...myyyy...gooolden aaarm?" It came again, a singsong of wailing and wheezing.

Eddy sat up in bed in a cold sweat.

Closer it came. (Pause.) It was right out his window. "Whooo's...got...myyyy... gooolden aaarm?"

He heard the window sill CRUNCH. (pause) He felt a bony hand upon his shoulder. "Whooo's...got...myyyy...gooolden aaarm?" (Say it sadly and accusingly. Stare intently off at someone in the audience. Give a long pause and let it build into a hush. Then jump suddenly at the person and yell.)

"DO YOU HAVE IT?"

© Stanley 2007. Reprinted with permission from *Florida Reading Quarterly*, Winter 2007.

Mini-Lesson #5: Repeating Line Story

Great memorable stories often have repeating lines, for example, "Run, run, as fast as you can. You can't catch me, I'm the Gingerbread Man!" Repeating lines, like a song's refrain, invite audience participation. Bob Dylan's "Blowin' in the Wind" is a good example of this: "The answer, my friend, is blowin' in the wind / The answer is blowin' in the wind."

Experience

1. Read and retell the story.
2. Teacher and students tell and read aloud other examples of repeating line stories. (See books with repeating lines at http://www.aacintervention.com/repeatl.htm.)

Reflect

1. Discuss the story on the next page, "I Wouldn't Let It Concern Me If I Were You" by Nile Stanley.
2. Do you think Bert Johnson was really a jinx? Why? Why not?
3. Why do so many stories have repeating lines? Can you name some favorites?
4. Do you know anyone that uses a repeating line? Are they trying to teach or trick?

Apply

1. Do a visual portrait of a story with a beginning, problem, solution, and end.
2. Tell and write your own repeating line story.
3. Read the lyrics to "I Am a Jinx" by Jeff Trippe, a song inspired by "I Wouldn't Let It Concern Me If I Were You" (lyrics printed after the story). Write a song about a story you have read. Use a traditional folk song melody and write new lyrics (e.g., "Down in the Valley," "Home on the Range").

Resources

http://www.songsforteaching.com/index.html
Songs for Teaching offers thousands of children's songs, lyrics, sound clips, and teaching suggestions.

http://www.cowboyfun.com/
Cowboy poetry and stories

http://www.folkstreams.net/film,39 (movie) and http://www.folkstreams.net/context,276 (teaching guide)
The film *Cowboy Poets* explains the cowboy-poetry tradition.

http://www.youtube.com/watch?v=tkL9PoOABPE
Cowboy poet Baxter Black tells the story, "Just a Dog."

http://www.youtube.com/watch?v=8B8wmVIuk2U
Cowboy singer Michael Martin Murphey sings "Vanishing Breed."

I Wouldn't Let It Concern Me If I Were You by Nile Stanley

When I lived in North Dakota I learned the cowboy way. My neighbor Bert Johnson had a 100-acre ranch with twenty-three horses. Bert wasn't a spring chicken so he'd ask me to lend a hand with chores. When his "ailments" would flare up, I'd help with mending fences, baling hay, breaking wild broncos, and even birthing foals. In exchange for all this he'd let me ride any of his twenty-three pride-and-joys. Now this sounds great, but there was one drawback. I know you won't believe this. Bert was a jinx, and something bad always happened when I was around him.

CRASH! I just spilled my coffee and broke my cup just thinking about the old timer. Don't worry I'll clean up this mess in a minute.
I wouldn't let it concern me if I were you.

One time after a big rainstorm I went over to Bert's to check on him. He said, "Rain really cooled things off. Why don't you give Miss Caddy some exercise."
"Awful muddy isn't it?" I said.
I wouldn't let it concern me if I were you.

Hesitant, down the muddy road I went. Caddy was frightened by the squishy mud under her feet and broke into a fast gallop. Caught off-guard by the sudden up-and-down motion of me bouncing like a super ball on her back, my feet came out of the stirrups and I pitched over Caddy's shoulder into the mud. She ran off in giddy terror.

"Where'd Miss Caddy go? What have you been doing, mud wrestling?" Bert asked me, when I arrived back at his house.
"She ran off, spooked by the mud," I replied.
I wouldn't let it concern me if I were you.

Another time, Bert asked me to help him put a halter on Miss Lazy Jane. She was running crazy in the yard in a real frothy frenzy. We cornered her against the electric fence. SNAP! She bolted into the air with a jolt, knocking me to the ground.

"Shouldn't we turn off the electric?" I asked.
I wouldn't let it concern me if I were you.

Another time, Bert was trying to get old Puddy Puss onto a horse trailer. She was real stubborn. Bribing her with sweet feed and carrots would not coax her in. Bert took out a whip.

I said, "I don't think that's a good idea."
I wouldn't let it concern me if I were you.

As he snapped her butt with the whip, old Puddy Puss jumped high in the air, crashing down, bending over the chain link fence like tinfoil.

Finally, one day it was hot, very hot, in fact it was 102 degrees. Bert called and said he needed help unloading a truck of alfalfa.

"I'm real busy at work today, besides what are you, crazy? It's 102 out there. Let's wait till it cools off."

I wouldn't let it concern me if I were you.

The next morning Bert's wife called and said, "It's over, he's been called home to the great pasture in the sky."

"What's that?"

"Dead, I said, of a heart attack!" She groaned.

"If only I helped him with that hay."

"I wouldn't let it concern me if I were you." She hung up.

That night I had trouble sleeping, thinking how Bert's sudden death was my fault. If I hadn't been so selfish. Then again, he was an awful jinx.

Very late, I thought I heard a knock at the door. Who could it be at this hour? I groggily got out of bed and opened the door. To my horror it was he, Bert Johnson. He was all dirty, made of skin and bones. In fact his skin was hanging off his bones. One eye was drooping out of the socket.

"For God's sake, Bert, you can't go walking around like that. You're a walking skeleton!"

I WOULDN'T LET IT CONCERN ME IF I WERE YOU!

© Stanley 2007

I Am a Jinx by Jeff Trippe (in the key of C)

🔘 **Hear It! Track #18**

```
G              C                    F
In old North Dakota, in the deep rollin' hills
G                    C                        G
Mid the songs of cicadas and the sweet whippoorwills,
G              C                    F
There dwelt an old cowboy we knew as old Bert,
        G7                      C
As thin as a whippet, as brown as the dirt.
```

Verse 2:
And the hands thereabouts said his luck was all bad,
His cattle were low and his horses were sad,
The hands thereabouts kept old Bert at arm's length,
For as he'd tell you himself, Bert was a jinx.

Chorus:
```
C          C7          F    G    C
"Friends, we all know it's true, I am a jinx,
C          G              G7    C
My biscuits are brittle, and my fiddlin' stinks,
   C7          F – D7      G          C - Am
My feet are both flat and my beard is all kinks,
     G      F     G7    C
And if that ain't enough, I am a jinx."
```

Verse 3:
Last month on a Monday, Bert drove into town,
To have a bad tooth divest of its crown,
When the dentist leaned over and got a whiff of Bert's breath,
His own teeth fell out, t'was a fate worse than death.

Chorus

Mini-lesson #6: Superhero Story

Since the dawn of storytelling we have had the need to be uplifted by fantasy tales of extraordinary superheroes, and superheroines. We need heroes in our world like Hercules, Helen of Troy, Superman, and Batgirl because they give us hope and someone to model ourselves after. Superheroes unselfishly fight the thugs and tackle the big problems we are either too afraid of or find a real inconvenience in our busy, self-centered lives. Recently, *Time* magazine listed *Watchmen*, a graphic novel about a ragbag of bizarre, damaged, retired superheroes, as one of the 100 best novels of the century. The **graphic novel,** a book that uses drawings and dialogue to tell a story but is longer than a traditional comic book, is one of the most exciting mediums for literature today. Graphic novels, like the Manga (Japanese comics) series *Naruto* and retold classics like **Beowulf** and *Macbeth*, are becoming increasingly popular, creating a groundswell of excitement and interest for literacy teachers who want to grab their students' attention.

This lesson focuses on how to write a superhero story. Here are some questions that will help your students design a superhero or supervillain, whether they're creating a graphic novel, heavy metal song, radio drama, or video game script:

- What is my superhero's age, gender, education, occupation, and outlook on life?
- What superpowers does my superhero have?
- How did he/she become super?
- Does my superhero have a secret identity?
- How does my superhero use his/her powers to solve problems?
- What is it about my superhero that will appeal to my audience?

"Spudbuster" is a heavy metal song about a comic book superhero by Nile Stanley and Ben Brenner. The song focuses on Spudbuster's major passion/goal in life, which is helping sofa spuds—kids who watch too much TV. Spudbuster is a good guy who teaches kids how to "turn down TV" and "turn up" reading, playing, exercising, and other healthy endeavors. Be sure to explain to younger students that the "Spudbuster" song is an excerpt, part of a larger work, and not a complete story with a beginning, problem, solution, and end.

Experience
1. Listen to "Spudbuster" (Track #16).
2. Listen again and follow along with the printed lyrics.
3. Students take turns acting like a rock star performing the song before a huge crowd.

Reflect
1. Have students discuss what they think about Spudbuster's message?
2. Brainstorm common elements of various superhero stories.
3. Break the class into groups and discuss what a graphic novel, movie, radio drama, or video game about Spudbuster might look and sound like.

Apply
1. Write and tell original superhero stories either individually or in groups.
2. Have students keep a journal for a week documenting how may hours daily they spend watching TV and playing video games.

3. Start a school-wide Spudbuster campaign to create media awareness and develop critical viewing skills. (There is a "TV Turnoff Week" in April and September. Visit http://www.tvturnoff.org/ for more information.)
4. Have a superhero costume contest where students show and tell why they are the most super.
5. Have students do book talks about their favorite graphic novels.

Resources

http://www.superheronation.com/2008/02/24/index-writing-about-superheroes/
"How to Write a Superhero Story"

http://www.readwritethink.org/lessons/lesson_view.asp?id=921
"The Comic Book Show and Tell" lesson from NCTE/IRA

http://www.adbusters.org/
Adbusters Media Foundation is a not-for-profit, anti-consumerist organization that publishes *AdBusters* magazine and works to change the way information is spread.

Spudbuster by Nile Stanley and Ben Brenner

 Hear It! Track #16

Hey all you sofa spuds,
Gather round.
The TV's blaring,
You're sittin' in a coma staring.
Turn down the TV
Cause it's spread'en VD (video disease).
Your brain is dead.
You got noth'en in your head.
Watch'en all that crud
Has made you into a sofa spud,
Made you into a sofa spud.

Spudbuster! Spudbuster! Spudbuster!

You're a slouch
On the couch,
A junk food junkie,
A first-grade flunkie.
You're wasting time
Stuck on that grime.
The only friends you met
Are stuck inside your TV set.
You gotta take a chance,
Gotta break the trance,
Break the trance.

Spudbuster! Spudbuster! Spudbuster!
Unplug the drug! Unplug the drug! Unplug the drug!
Don't become a sofa spud!

He's gonna disable your cable,
Remove your remote.
Hope you can cope.
Toss Nintendo out the window.
Lock up your Xbox.
Read a book and take a look.
Ride a bike and take a hike.
Cut your IV from the TV.
Make a choice and raise your voice.
And click on me and set yourself free.Click on me and set yourself free.

Spudbuster! Spudbuster! Spudbuster!

Resources

IRA and NCTE Standards Addressed
by Storytelling and Story Writing

Storytelling and story writing address numerous standards. The following are the joint International Reading Association (IRA) and National Council of Teachers of English (NCTE) standards. Every mini-lesson addresses standards 1, 3, 4, 5, 6, 11, and 12. When the teacher goes beyond the basic mini-lesson plan using the suggested resources, activities, culturally responsive literature, multimedia, and content-area connections, all of these standards are addressed.

1. Students read a wide range of print and non-print texts to build an understanding of texts, of themselves, and of the cultures of the United States and the world; to acquire new information; to respond to the needs and demands of society and the workplace; and for personal fulfillment. Among these texts are fiction and non-fiction, classic and contemporary works.

2. Students read a wide range of literature from many periods in many genres to build an understanding of the many dimensions (e.g., philosophical, ethical, aesthetic) of human experience.

3. Students apply a wide range of strategies to comprehend, interpret, evaluate, and appreciate texts. They draw on their prior experience, their interactions with other readers and writers, their knowledge of word meaning and of other texts, their word identification strategies, and their understanding of textual features (e.g., sound-letter correspondence, sentence structure, context, graphics).

4. Students adjust their use of spoken, written, and visual language (e.g., conventions, style, vocabulary) to communicate effectively with a variety of audiences and for different purposes.

5. Students employ a wide range of strategies as they write and use different writing process elements appropriately to communicate with different audiences for a variety of purposes.

6. Students apply knowledge of language structure, language conventions (e.g., spelling and punctuation), media techniques, figurative language, and genre to create, critique, and discuss print and non-print texts.

7. Students conduct research on issues and interests by generating ideas and questions, and by posing problems. They gather, evaluate, and synthesize data from a variety of sources (e.g., print and non-print texts, artifacts, people) to communicate their discoveries in ways that suit their purpose and audience.

8. Students use a variety of technological and information resources (e.g., libraries, databases, computer networks, video) to gather and synthesize information and to create and communicate knowledge.

9. Students develop an understanding of and respect for diversity in language use, patterns, and dialects across cultures, ethnic groups, geographic regions, and social roles.

10. Students whose first language is not English make use of their first language to develop competency in the English language arts and to develop understanding of content across the curriculum.

11. Students participate as knowledgeable, reflective, creative, and critical members of a variety of literacy communities.
12. Students use spoken, written, and visual language to accomplish their own purposes (e.g. for learning, enjoyment, persuasion, and the exchange of information).

Five Pillars of Reading Addressed by Storytelling and Story Writing

In 2000, the National Reading Panel (NRP) advocated a comprehensive approach to literacy instruction. Storytelling enhances your standards-based instruction with phonemic awareness, phonics, fluency, vocabulary, and comprehension:

Phonemic Awareness
- Identify rhyming words heard in stories and song.
- Change voice pitch, tone and intonation to differentiate characters and produce sound effects.
- Chant and sing repeating refrains in stories and songs.

Phonics
- Identify rhyming words read in stories and lyrics.
- Track voice to print match by following along with a pointer as a story is orally read.
- Teach target letter–sound relationships with word study during the reading of connected text.
- Help learners concentrate on sound–symbol correspondences through spelling and writing activities.

Fluency
- Read aloud, choral-read, and perform reader's theater of stories.
- Read selected sight word and sight word phrases from stories.
- Develop fluent oral language production by telling stories with guided instruction on volume, pronunciation, and expression.
- Develop written fluency through learning "to write talk down." What the student can tell, the student can write.

Vocabulary
- Define and use the language of storytelling (e.g. folktale, cumulative tale, problem, resolution, metaphor, and personification).
- Use context clues to define and understand difficult vocabulary in stories.
- Increase listening, speaking, reading, and writing vocabularies with immersion in narratives in print and non-print mediums.
- Learn the literary language and patterns of stories: form, structure, cadence, and rhythm.
- Use vocabulary by incorporating it into stories that students hear, act out, retell, read, and write.

Comprehension
- Recall key story elements by oral, written, and pictorial retellings.
- Demonstrate knowledge of story patterns and literary devices by using them in the writing of original stories.

- Increase cultural and multicultural literacy by understanding the cultural, historical, and social context of stories.
- Use the five "W's" to remember important story details.
- Listen and read a wide variety of stories using questioning and discussion strategies.

A note from the authors: We encourage teachers to use their professional judgment when using storytelling to teach distinct skills. There's always the danger of the "skills" becoming more important than the storytelling—putting the cart before the horse. We recommend balancing the holistic approach with the skills approach. The skills are not the end, but the means. All too often, the teaching of the skills has interfered with students becoming enthusiastic, engaged readers and writers.

Storytelling Curriculum Tie-ins

Because storytelling is an integral part of the way we approach learning, it's an important facilitator for learning in most areas of study in the school curriculum. Listed below are but a few suggestions to help integrate storytelling into your classroom activities.

Art
- Analyze stories for use of strong imagery and visual details.
- Use stories to develop themes.
- Use stories that create patterns or rhythms and translate them into visual patterns.
- Use stories to motivate and stimulate creativity.
- Suggested resources:
  - ➤ *Uncle Andy's: A Faabbbulous Visit with Andy Warhol* by James Warhola
  - ➤ *Suzette and the Puppy: A Story about Mary Cassatt* by Joan Sweeney
  - ➤ *Pablo Picasso: Breaking All the Rules* by True Kelley
  - ➤ *Life Doesn't Frighten Me* by Maya Angelou
  - ➤ *Degas and the Little Dancer* by Laurence Anholt

Geography and Social Studies
- Tell or listen to stories that show the way of life, customs, and beliefs of an area or ethnic group.
- Incorporate stories into the curriculum that explain the why and how of the earth's formation.
- Use stories that have geographical details in the setting.
- When studying West African or Jamaican cultures, listen to Anansi stories and then discuss how these stories reflect the cultural identity of the people.
- Suggested resources:
  - ➤ *Discovering World Geography with Books Kids Love* by Nancy Chicola and Eleanor B. English
  - ➤ *The Story of the World* by Susan Wise Bauer
  - ➤ *Jamaican Folk Tales and Oral Histories* by Laura Tanna
  - ➤ *The Origin of Life on Earth: An African Creation Myth* by David A. Anderson

History

- Use stories that are based on historical events.
- Analyze details of stories that show cause and effect.
- Use biographical stories.
- Suggested resources:
  - ➤ *Black Wings: Courageous Stories of African Americans in Aviation and Space History* by Von Hardesty
  - ➤ *If a Bus Could Talk: The Story of Rosa Parks* by Faith Ringgold
  - ➤ *Jane Goodall: A Biography* by Meg Greene
  - ➤ *Many Rides of Paul Revere* by James Cross Giblin
  - ➤ *The Snow Baby: The Arctic Childhood of Robert E. Peary's Daring Daughter* by Katherine Kirkpatrick
  - ➤ *The Storyteller's Candle/La Velita de los Cuentos*, by Lucia Gonzalez and Lulu Delacre
  - ➤ *Zora Hurston and the Chinaberry Tree* by William Miller, Cornelius Van Wright, and Ying-Hwa Hu

Literature

- Use stories to enhance and reinforce vocabulary development.
- Tell or listen to stories that provide examples of how literary elements are used effectively.
- Use stories to motivate and stimulate interest in reading and writing (see the Index of Suggested Stories by Story Type in the back of this book).

Math

- When teaching how to solve word problems, turn arithmetic equations into stories.
- Look for stories that include problem solving, inference, sequencing, and patterns.
- Use stories that make comparisons and show cause and effect.
- Suggested resources:
  - ➤ Math story problems for grades 1-6: http://edhelper.com/WordStories. htm, http://www.mathplayground.com/wpdatabase/wpindex.html, and http://www.mathstories.com/
  - ➤ Kid-created story problems from Math Cats: http://www.mathcats.com/ storyproblems.html
  - ➤ *40 Fabulous Math Mysteries Kids Can't Resist (Grades 4-8)* by Marcia Miller and Martin Lee

Music

- Choreograph stories.
- Compose songs to go with the stories.
- Compose music to tell the story.
- Suggested resources:
  - ➤ Karaoke player and a variety of songs
  - ➤ VanBasco Karaoke Player (free): http://www.vanbasco.com/ karaokeplayer/
  - ➤ *The Story of the Orchestra: Listen While You Learn about the Instruments, the Music and the Composers Who Wrote the Music!* by Robert Levine
  - ➤ *Sing My Song: A Kid's Guide to Songwriting* by Steve Seskin

> *Sing Like the Stars* by Roger Love

> *I've Been Burping in the Classroom and Other Silly Sing-Along Songs* by Bruce Lansky

Science

- For a unit on scientific theory, look for "how" and "why" stories such as "Why Raven's Feathers Are Black" and "How the Leopard Got Its Spots."
- For a unit on the rain forests, look at stories from or about the indigenous peoples of Brazil.
- To teach analyzing skills, use stories that show cause and effect or that make comparisons.
- Suggested resources:
  > *How We Know What We Know About Our Changing Climate: Scientists and Kids Explore Global Warming* by Lynne Cherry and Gray Braasch
  > *Midnight Forests: A Story of Gifford Pinchot and Our National Forests* by Gary Hines
  > *Midnight Forests: A Story of Gifford Pinchot and Our National Forests* by Gary Hines
  > *The Telephone Gambit: Chasing Alexander Graham Bell's Secret* by Seth Shulman

Standards from http://www.tampastory.org/tsf_append.htm#standards, © 1998 Tampa-Hillsborough County Storytelling Festival Committee

Companion Website

A companion website, http://www.unf.edu/~nstanley/links.htm, offers additional teaching tips and helpful resources, including:

- **Documentaries about storytelling**
  > ***Magic of Performance Literacy*** (13 minutes, RealPlayer). Reading professor and performance poet Nile Stanley and storyteller Brett Dillingham use the magic of performance literacy at Riverbend Elementary School in Juneau, Alaska.
  > ***Autumn Leaves*** (26 minutes, RealPlayer). Storyteller Brett Dillingham does performance literacy at Stepping Stones Pupil Referral Unit, Cauderdale Council, in Halifax, England. The school is for students with learning and emotional disabilities who have not succeeded in the mainstream classroom. Watch as children with challenges are transformed through storytelling and become engaged in productive language and literacy.
- **Digital storytelling and poetry presentations**
- **Articles**
- **Interviews with authors, storytellers, and poets**

Techniques to Try

Night of a Living Wax Museum

Living wax museums bring to life important and amazing people through the power of performance. Many variations of this creative technique are possible, but the general idea is to put on a performance for parents in which students dress up as historical figures, stand perfectly still, and come alive only when approached by a parent visitor. A narrator with a flashlight leads parents through a dark library as students stand motionless, dressed in period costumes within authentic-looking sets. As the narrator shines the light on each figure, the characters spring to life, telling his tales and answering questions. Student PowerPoint presentations after the museum tour enrich the audience's understanding of each historic figure's early life, education, challenges overcome, and societal contributions.

Students' work can be evaluated by using a rubric for each of these components:
1. Select an important figure in history.
2. Read and research the figure.
3. Write a script and brief report.
4. Create a period costume and set.
5. Role-play that person in the "Night of a Living Wax Museum" performance.

Here are some adaptations of this idea that were very successful:
- An arts magnet school presented a living wax exhibit for a Black History celebration. Louis "Satchmo" Armstrong sang and held his trumpet; a mustachioed Langston Hughes recited poetry; and Zora Lee Hurston told tall tales while wearing a feather boa.
- Another school did an exhibit of famous scientists and their inventions.
- An art teacher had students become different artists and depict different styles of art, including Picasso and Cubism, Norman Rockwell and Realism, and Mary Cassat and Impressionism.
- A fifth-grade after-school book club hosted an eerie tour of famous Americans Paul Revere, Harriet Tubman, Betsy Ross, and Thomas Jefferson. This history lesson, in which students presented biographies as story theatre, culminated in a grand finale appearance by Lady Liberty herself, the Statue of Liberty.

Interview with a Crocodile

Pretending to be an expert helps children actually become one. In "Interview with a Crocodile," children become any animal, person, or even object that they have studied. They tell their stories through a class question-and-answer session. Knowledge is obtained through peer interaction, and the cooperative exchange between expert (the teller) and novice (the listener) is mutually beneficial. The teller learns how to research, take notes, remember important facts and vocabulary, and express knowledge in a creative way. The listener learns how to learn, problem-solve, and conduct research through the interview. There is pragmatic value, as the children learn to have a conversation as if they were learned people on the job working together to solve real-world problems.

This technique is a variation of the widely used K-W-L Reading Comprehension Strategy ("What do I know? What do I want to know? What did I learn?") (Ogle, 1986).

Take a look at how the activity might play out in science class.

Listener: "Where do you live, Mr. Crocodile?"
Teller: "I live in a habitat that is swampy and warm. I really like Africa."

Listener: "How big do crocodiles get?"
Teller: "Big enough to eat you! Seriously, the Nile Crocodile can grow to sixteen or even twenty feet."

Listener: "How long do crocodiles live?"
Teller: "Very long. Some live to be sixty or even one-hundred."

Listener: "How can you tell an alligator from a crocodile?"
Teller: "The easiest way to tell the difference between the two is that a crocodile has a very long, narrow, V-shaped snout, while the alligator's snout is wider and U-shaped."

Listener: "What's another difference?"
Teller: "I am not sure, but I will get back to you with more information after I do some more research."

I Was There
"I Was There" is a technique for presenting historical content through the voices of ordinary people, such as your students. It is a form of oral history in which students use their imaginations to observe and participate in significant social events from their reading. It asks the student to get up close and personal with a topic. Mary Pope Osborne's *Magic Tree House* series combines this storytelling technique with learning facts about geography and history. In this series, eight-year-old Jack and his seven-year-old sister use a magic tree house filled with books to whirl away to faraway places and times. Imagine just pointing at a book's picture and ZING—you're there with the pilgrims celebrating the first Thanksgiving. Or ZING—you're in Camelot helping Merlin the Magician. Reading aloud from this book may help students to understand the first-person point-of-view narration.

"I Was There" is a creative and fun alternative to the boring book report. The procedure is easy. Have students read about a significant event. Encourage reading from trade biography books. Students then use the five Ws to summarize the key elements of the event. They should think about their personal reaction to the event and take an emotional stance. Students can blend the retelling with some personal narrative or make up a story about how they came to be at an event.

Digital Storytelling

What Is Digital Storytelling?
Digital storytelling is the practice of using computer-based tools to tell stories. Digital stories usually contain some mixture of computer-based images, text, recorded audio narration, video clips, and music. In this section, we discuss two approaches to digital storytelling (Ohler, 2008):
   1. Digitally enhanced oral storytelling (DEOST), our performance literacy process integrated with technology, in which students perform stories live in front of a green screen and add images behind their performances during post-production
   2. Computer-based digital storytelling (CBDS), which typically consists of combining voice-over narration with video and/or still images and music into short movies that are viewed via computer

Digital stories can vary in length, but most of the stories created by students are between one and ten minutes. They can range from personal tales, to visually compelling "show-and-tells" backed with a musical beat, to the recounting of historical events with a blend of personal interviews and news reel footage, to the retelling of favorite children's books with hand-sculpted clay figures. Telling stories through digital media has become easier and does not require expensive equipment or technological expertise. A variety of software applications, some of which are already on most computers (such as PowerPoint, iMovie, Movie Maker, and Photo Story), are commonly used.

The real hook for students is that digital storytelling gives them the ability to reach and connect with larger audiences. Publishing stories on the Web via YouTube, Facebook, and podcasts is very easy and has become a common practice in our culture and much of the world. Of benefit for educators is that students who engage in digital storytelling improve their literacy through planning, creating, orally sharing ideas and stories, writing, reading, narrating, and illustrating.

What Is Digitally Enhanced Oral Storytelling?
Digital storytelling has garnered a great deal of excitement in the past decade as a way to enhance storytelling while teaching modern technological skills. We have created digital storytelling projects with Alaska Natives, in Irish schools, with undergraduate and graduate students in education, and with inner-city populations in the southern United States. No matter the group or location, digital storytelling captivates, engages, and educates.

The simplest, most powerful way to begin digital storytelling is by taking the performance literacy process and integrating technology into it. When students write their own stories and then enhance with technology, you can be assured that they are experiencing powerful, contextual literacy that is motivating and meaningful.

When the students have finished their visual portrait of the story (VPS), telling/retelling, and writing, have them illustrate four pictures of events within the story that they think are important. Suggest they choose something relating to the beginning, problem, solution, and end. Let them know that these pictures are going to be scanned into a computer and later will be the background for their story in its final digital format. You may be surprised to find out that many students are aware of this process—they know that when they watch Iron Man or Harry Potter flying they are really pretending while actually being held up by a wire in front of a blue or green screen! The background is "placed" behind them later using software. Standard 8½ x 11 inch paper is fine for their illustrations; we suggest you use thick, white paper.

When the students perform their storytelling for a live audience, the background should be a green or blue wall (you can also rent or buy large, portable screens). Paint is cheap and finding a wall in your school that you can paint an 8 x 10 foot section of (the gym, library, large classroom) is often easy.

Before the audience arrives, set up a digital video camera on a tripod and have a handless, cordless (lavalier) microphone available—preferably two. They sound much better than the built-in microphones on cameras and free up your students' hands while they tell their stories. Having two microphones also guarantees that there is no "down time" between storytellers.

Your students should practice both 1) using the camera and 2) putting the microphone on and taking it off. As the audience comes in and sits down, they will see the camera ready to go and the tech students on standby. They will think something important is about to happen—and it is! You can either have video and sound "experts" who do all the taping/recording or let everyone take a turn at it. We suggest you have a few do it—those students who really want to work with the technology and will enjoy it. They can even teach you!

When your students have told and recorded their stories, they are ready to add the digital layers. This consists of scanning their illustrations into a computer, then taking the audio/video recordings and placing the drawings "behind" the tellers' video, replacing the green or blue background with their own artwork. Have some of your students who are really good at it train others in scanning their pictures and dropping them behind their digital stories. This way they all learn some very useful and interesting skills. The technology and software to do this will change over time, but the concept of digitizing artwork and creating their own backgrounds will remain.

Your students will be amazed to see and hear their stories on a computer with the backgrounds they created themselves placed at appropriate times in their stories. It is even more impressive if you get a hold of an LCD projector with external speakers and play it on a white screen or wall. It looks and feels like a Hollywood production—that is, a Hollywood production with a good story!

For an example of performance-based, green-screen storytelling, watch "Fox Becomes a Better Person," performed by fourth-grader Hannah Davis: http://www. youtube.com/watch?v=Bw4lEdsd_fo. You'll see how a chroma (green) screen, scanned picture, and original picture were all used as backgrounds.

Who Is The Audience?
The storytelling we have shared with you so far has been geared towards live audiences. The advantage of digital storytelling is that students can post their stories on Facebook or YouTube for free (YouTube has a ten-minute limit on length of videos) for anyone with an Internet connection to see anywhere in the world. They can also burn copies on DVDs and give them to relatives and friends or share them with classes of children anywhere in the world that have the capability to watch them.

The Digitally Enhanced Oral Storytelling Process

1) Show an example of a digital storytelling to the class. Ideally it is one the teacher created—that way she knows the entire process! Make sure the class has already created their own performance literacy storytelling so they are aware of the importance of integrating sound, expression, and movement.

2) Ask the class what was different about the digital storytelling from the other types of storytelling they are used to.

3) Create a visual portrait of the story that reflects the story you just told so your students see that digital storytelling also uses the VPS as a foundation for the creation of their stories.

4) Brainstorm subjects for your students to write about that fit your curriculum.

5) Brainstorm problems and solutions directly relating to the subject ideas your students just suggested. Here is an example:

WALRUS	
PROBLEM	**SOLUTION**
Attacked by Killer Whale	Uses his tusks to climb up on ice
Hungry	Finds school of fish in kelp bed
Pollution from oil spill	Swims far away; loses family
Water getting too warm	Humans stop global warming
Pup gets lost	Finds another walrus mother

6) Pass out 11" x 17" paper and give your students ten to fifteen minutes to create their own VPS. Make sure you walk around and prompt those who need it with questions about their subject, problem, or solution.

7) Model telling/retelling one of your students' stories once the VPS is finished.

8) In pairs, have your students practice telling/retelling their stories.

9) Have your students do a fast-write of their stories. Give them ten to twenty minutes for this.

10) Ask a student to tell his story in front of the class. Model how to critique with questions, such as "What did I do to make this a good storytelling?" and "What could I do to make it even better?" Do this two or three more times, making sure students use specific suggestions (sound, expression, and movement critiques).

11) In groups of three to five, have students tell stories and critique in different parts of the room.

12) Pass out 8½" x 11" paper and have your students illustrate four scenes from their story. Suggest that they choose scenes from their beginning, problem, solution, and end. They should turn their paper sideways because it looks more like a computer screen and scans better that way. Remind them that these pictures will be the "scenes" behind their digital storytelling. They should place the main picture off-center because the center piece will be the teller in the video. You may choose to let your students use photographs (ones they take or own already) where appropriate or pictures they download from the Internet. This would be a great time to teach them about copyright and asking permission to use someone else's work.

13) Have your students tell their stories and repeat the critiquing process in front of entire class. At this stage they will be very supportive of each other's storytelling.

14) Students scan in the pictures or photos they have that go with their stories.

15) Using iMovie, Movie Maker, or other software, students overlay their live storytelling over their pictures/photos.
16) Watch some of the stories on computers or using an LCD projector. Burn copies of the entire class's storytelling on DVDs and give copies to each student. Publish for the school board, assemblies, YouTube, Facebook, etc.
17) Invite other classes, parents, and community members to the storytelling event. This is the time students tell their stories in front of a blue or green screen and other students videotape and audio record the telling.

For all the technical details and a step-by-step process using green or blue screen digital video storytelling, we highly recommend Dr. Jason Ohler's website: http://www.jasonohler.com/storytelling/storytech.cfm.

Other Ideas for Computer-based Digital Storytelling

The Music Video

A Jacksonville, Florida sixth-grade class had a global studies project with a focus on Latin America. The class partnered with a sixth-grade class in Buenos Aires, Argentina in order to have a cultural exchange. The Jacksonville students wanted to tell the students in Argentina a little about themselves and decided to tell the story of their lives digitally. They brought in pictures and wrote list poems. They used Movie Maker because they were more familiar with that program and it was easier to time the slides with the music.

Their teacher showed them a powerful music video her professor had showed in her college class. The video was for "We Didn't Start the Fire," the 1989 hit song and video by Billy Joel (http://www.youtube.com/watch?v=pKu2QaytmrM). It makes reference to a catalog of headline events (e.g., the Sputnik launch, Bay of Pigs Invasion, assassination of President Kennedy) that occurred during Joel's lifetime. It's both a great history lesson and a wonderful example of digital storytelling at its best. The catchy tune and list-poem format of this hit have spawned numerous parodies including an episode of The Simpsons and a Coca-Cola commercial in Latin America. It also caught the attention of the aspiring student writers. They took Joel's chorus and historical list of events and changed them to fit their lives.

For another example of a digitized "show-and–tell" story, view "Black History," an animated, hip-hop history by Miller Boyz: http://www.youtube.com/watch?v=yRw6ypld_3g.

Claymation

A third-grade media specialist was intrigued with claymation. Some of the best-known, clay-animated works include the *Gumby* television series, popular films such as *Chicken Run* and *Wallace & Gromit*, and the children's show *Bob the Builder*.

In clay animation, which is one of the many forms of stop-motion animation, each character is sculpted in clay or a similarly pliable material such as Plasticine. The characters are arranged on the set (background), a film frame is taken and the character is then moved slightly by hand. Another frame is taken and the character is moved slightly again. This cycle is repeated until the animator has achieved the desired amount of film. Producing a stop-motion animation using clay is extremely laborious. Typically, twelve camera shots are needed for one second of film movement.

Claymation makers produce their animated story frames with computer software. Claymation Studio from Honest Technology is one example of software that uses images from a digital camera, webcam, or DV camcorder. First, the storytellers come up with an idea for a character, props, and a background. With this information, they create a storyboard for the idea of the movie. The storyboard includes the basic layout of the sequence of events. Next, the characters are developed with clay. Digital photos are taken. Computer software is used to animate the stop-action pictures. Students add narration and a soundtrack, as well as a title page and credits. The final claymation can be be burned to a DVD or posted on YouTube. Check with your school's media specialist for upcoming competitions in which your students can enter their claymation films. Winning an award is a great incentive.

For detailed how-tos, visit
The Clay Animation Station at http://library.thinkquest.org/22316/home.html.

You can find several claymation adaptations of favorite stories by doing a YouTube search.

PowerPoint
A kindergarten class loved reading their favorite animal stories by award-winning children's authors and watching animated versions online:
- Mo Williams' *Knuffle Bunny*: http://www.pigeonpresents.com/pals-knuffle.aspx
- Ezra Jack Keats' *Maggie and the Pirate*: http://www.ezra-jack-keats.org/kids/index.html
- Norman Bridwell's *Clifford the Big Red Dog* Interactive Storybooks: http://teacher.scholastic.com/clifford1/index.htm

After watching many digital stories they wanted to compose their own. Some of the children composed original animal stories. Others extended stories they had read by writing sequels to their favorite children's books. They then scanned their original drawings and narrated their stories by using PowerPoint.

Movie Maker and YouTube
Windows Movie Maker is easy to use and comes already installed on many PCs. You can use the Google Image search engine to find free, non-copyrighted pictures that support your narratives, or record performances with a digital video camera. Download the videos to Movie Maker, use a microphone to do voice-over narration where necessary, and add music (either free downloads or original songs if you're musically inclined). Final stories can be published on YouTube. There are plenty of examples at the companion website: http://www.unf.edu/~nstanley/powerpoint.htm.

More Examples and Links
- "Raven Day." Storyteller Brett Dillingham tells a transformation tale of animal magic: http://www.youtube.com/watch?v=wvTrd-vUDxQ
- "How Drum Learned to Talk." Nile Stanley tells a pourquoi story, or creation tale: http://www.youtube.com/watch?v=-K7A_dX504s

- "Climbing the Poet-tree." Karen Alexander raps about rhymes: http://www. youtube.com/watch?v=GzUYOsauY6Q
- For more on software and Web tools, visit http://mikefisher.wikispaces.com/ TopTenTools and http://mikefisher.wikispaces.com/DS+Web+Tools

What Are the Benefits of Digital Storytelling?

There are many types of digital storytelling that address multiple literacies. Here are some specific benefits:

Personal expression. Students harness the power of story to define their identities, share their ideas and ideals, entertain, inform and influence larger audiences, and often heal and transform their communities. By adding the digital component to storytelling, students acquire even more tools to magnify their voices and extend them to the global stage.

Literary connection. Many children's book authors have digitized their stories. E-books and animated stories are appealing to kids—many of these are children who grew up with a computer mouse in hand. New life has been breathed into old tales with multimedia. Ask a kid, "Have you read the *Polar Express*?" Most will say, "Yeah, I read it after I saw the movie with Tom Hanks."

Media literacy. To do digital storytelling well, students learn the skills needed for success in the 21st century: how to use the computer, software, the Internet, a digital camera, a scanner, microphones, and more.

Cooperative learning. Students work together. They read and revise each other's work. The more capable students support the less skilled, particularly in the use of technology.

Literacy. At every step of the digital storytelling process, students are learning and performing literacy. In choosing a topic for a story, they are brainstorming. With content-related stories, such as historical accounts, students use research skills. In creating the narrative script, there is the use of the visual portrait or graphic organizer, retelling, summarizing, writing, editing, and revising. Honing a story involves word choice and vocabulary development, as well as the skillful use of a variety of literary devices such as metaphor and personification. Performing a story builds communication skills (listening and speaking), reading fluency, and comprehension. The story mini-lessons provide detailed examples of how the skills and standards of literacy are developed through storytelling.

Standards reinforcement. In today's educational climate, classroom instruction must be correlated with local, state, or even national standards. It is clear that to meet the challenges of the 21st century, teachers and students need digital-age skills. These resources show the clear link between digital storytelling and the standards:
- American Association of School Librarians (AASL) Standards for the 21st-Century Learner: http://www.ala.org/ala/mgrps/divs/aasl/aaslproftools/ learningstandards/AASL_Learning_Standards_2007.pdf
- International Society for Technology in Education (ISTE) National Educational Technology Standards (NETS): http://www.iste.org/AM/ Template.cfm?Section=NETS

- International Reading Association (IRA)/National Council of Teachers of English (NCTE) Standards for the English Language Arts: http://www.readwritethink.org/standards/

Digital Storytelling Mini-Lesson: Two Stories about Ourselves
(Developed by Jason Ohler with Experience-Reflect-Apply contributions from Nile Stanley and Brett Dillingham)

This pair of stories helps students understand their pasts and create the futures they want. The first story is "Who Am I and How Did I Get Here?" This focuses on an important event in students' lives that help explain "where they are at" today.

The second story is "Becoming a Hero of Your Own Future Life." This story focuses on students identifying the kind of person they would like to be or the kind of lifestyle or job they would like to have. Of particular interest in story two is the kind of personal changes students need to undergo in order to reach their goals.

Both stories lend themselves to the digital storytelling methods described in this chapter.

Story #1: "Who Am I and How Did I Get Here?"

Experience
The story metaphor for this story is "the autobiographical documentary." The goal is for students to do more than just report the event. Instead, as narrators, they need to explain how the event changed them and contributed to their understanding of themselves. Teachers can model this by telling their own stories about events that changed them or by telling stories about important events that happened to people they know.

Reflect
Teachers direct students to recall a particular event that has meaning for them. It could be anything, including a family outing, a personal tragedy, a successful adventure, or moving from one town to another, to name a few. Next, teachers direct students to identify what they learned from it or how it changed them. Students reflect this understanding through writing or sketching a visual portrait of the story.

Apply
Students use elements of performance literacy to prepare and perform their stories (DEOST—digitally enhanced oral storytelling) or to prepare and speak their oral narration (CBDS—computer-based digital storytelling). Both approaches (Ohler, 2008) will require the production or preparation of personal images. In the case of DEOST, the images will appear behind the recorded performance in the final production of the video. In the case of CBDS, the images will appear on the computer screen, supporting the narration. Images can be scanned photos and objects, original artwork, or digital photos. For example, a student might use a scan of an old photo of a family member or a personal artifact like a medal, an old

wallet, or a locket of hair. Students might also create their own artwork, take digital photos, or, in more technically advanced situations, create or adapt video footage.

Story #2: "Becoming a Hero of Your Own Future Life"

Experience

The story metaphor for this story is "the hero quest story." As such, it is built upon the "story core," which condenses Joseph Campbell's *The Hero's Journey* into a basic thesis: Stories are about characters who address the challenges in their lives through personal transformation. A teacher can model this by telling a story about an accomplishment in her life—perhaps becoming a teacher. She should tell the story in terms of first deciding she wanted to become a teacher and how she reached this goal by evolving—in this case, learning lots of new and interesting things at school, learning how to listen to and work with people, or whatever she wants to highlight.

What if a student wants to be a bear? Or a mountain? Or captain of a spaceship? Or any other persona that uses a first-person magical point of view? Absolutely fine. The key is getting students to talk about why they seek this for themselves and how they need to change and grow in order to reach their goal. For example, if a student wants to be a bear because he wants to be a hunter or live in the forest, then his story would involve learning the hunting or outdoor life skills he would need in order to be successful. Suppose a student wanted to be a mountain so she could share the beautiful view she has of the surrounding land with others. In that case, her story might involve developing the sharing skills she needed to be the kind of mountain she envisions. And of course a spaceship captain needs just about every skill we see in an idealized hero, including courage, sound judgment, intelligence, and compassion. Telling a story about developing any of these qualities has great potential.

The important point is that the quest begins with a goal that is only reached because the hero changes or grows in ways that facilitate his success. The result is that students tell stories about being heroes of their own future lives.

Reflect

To stimulate reflection, teachers can ask students: Who do you want to be in three years? Five years? When you grow up? Is there someone you admire who you really want to be like? Have you ever seen someone doing something and said to yourself, "I want to do that for a living!" After students have identified who they want to be, they need to identify what they need to learn or how they need to change in order to become that person. This can include learning new things, "growing up," learning how to get along better with others—any kind of transformation that can serve as an individualized evolution plan, or IEP.

Apply

Similar to the first story, students use elements of performance literacy to prepare and perform their stories (DEOST approach) or to prepare and speak their oral narration (CBDS approach). All of the issues related to producing and including images described for the first story apply here.

Standards Addressed

- **AASL Standards for the 21st-Century Learner**
  - ➤ 1.42: Use interaction with and feedback from teachers and peers to guide own inquiry process.
  - ➤ 4.43: Recognize how to focus efforts in personal learning.
- **ISTE National Educational Technology Standards**
  - ➤ Students apply digital tools to gather, evaluate, and use information.
- **IRA/NCTE Standards for the English Language Arts**
  - ➤ Students adjust their use of spoken, written, and visual language (e.g., conventions, style, vocabulary) to communicate effectively with a variety of audiences and for different purposes.
  - ➤ Students conduct research on issues and interests by generating ideas and questions, and by posing problems. They gather, evaluate, and synthesize data from a variety of sources (e.g., print and non-print texts, artifacts, people) to communicate their discoveries in ways that suit their purpose and audience.

Storyteller's Name _____

Name of Story _____

Digital Storytelling Rubric

	Excellent	Good	Fair	Needs Work
Story	4	3	2	1

Is the story engaging, with an interesting beginning, problem, solution, and end?

Detail	4	3	2	1

Is the story told with enough detail to be coherent?

Point of View	4	3	2	1

Does the story have a clear purpose and point of view?

Narration	4	3	2	1

Is the voice narration clear and does it match the story line? Does it flow well with the content and images?

Pacing	4	3	2	1

Does the pacing of the narrative keep the audience engaged?

Grammar and Language Use	4	3	2	1

Are grammar and language use correct and appropriate for the telling of this particular story?

Images	4	3	2	1

Are the background images high quality and appropriately coordinated with the different scenes in the story?

Music	4	3	2	1

Does the music match the story line and tone?

Professionalism	4	3	2	1

Does the author have a title and credits page? Does the credits page contain appropriate reference citations/permission for any copyrighted material?

Technology Pitfalls

We've come to the same conclusion as digital storytelling expert and author Jason Ohler (2008, p.6): "All technology is an amplifier...and what happens when you give a bad guitar player a bigger amplifier? Ouch!" That is to say, we have been part of incredible digital storytelling projects that any teacher, parent, or community member would be proud of, but we have also witnessed others (not by our students!) that left us with the same feeling one gets from a Hollywood movie that concentrated on special effects only to let bad acting, empty dialog, and a weak story ruin the film. No technology or special effects can replace a well developed story complete with literary elements and personal voice.

That being said, technology can enhance a story. Digital storytelling software is increasingly being marketed to schools. Sales pitches on shiny boxes proclaim all your students have to do to produce a great digital story is point and click with the tools provided. Just choose and grab from a menu of prefabricated characters, plots, backgrounds, images, and soundtracks and, like magic, you create a masterpiece. We think that young children especially benefit more from a free exploration of materials and the freedom to create their own unique stories than they do if they are asked to attempt to re-create a story with images and music someone else has chosen for them.

Thus we caution teachers who may wish to "cut corners" using solely multimedia kits, clip art, and CD-ROMs full of images, royalty-free music, etc. This type of "cookie cutter" approach to digital storytelling is easier and less time consuming than creating stories from brainstorming, personal artwork, taking original photographs, doing video and sound, finding photos/pictures on the Internet, and learning about copyright laws and procedures. (The concept of educational fair use may be openly discussed in some schools—this provides students latitude in choosing the materials they may use. Other schools may have restrictions on what specific types of content may be used by students.)

However, by cutting corners, your students will miss developing their speaking and listening skills through telling and retelling with partners, higher-level thinking skills through drawing their own pictures or choosing relevant graphics, kinesthetic learning by performing for a live audience, etc. We feel a teacher would be selling the education of their students short and that most of the motivating factors inherent in the more educationally appropriate forms of digital storytelling are compromised by the "canned" approaches to creating and performing digital media. Let the story drive the technology.

Dealing with Technology Challenges

➤ **Lack of access.** Access to digital hardware and software varies greatly from school to school. Some schools seem to have it all, while others can't find funding to fix leaky roofs or replace broken windows, much less purchase state-of-the-art computers, video cameras, etc. We can't change the technologies a given school has at its disposal, but we suggest that whatever resources you have, use them in such a way that technology is naturally integrated into the curriculum via storytelling in ways that are meaningful and sensible.

If you have one computer that is less than three years old, one video camera (it can even be a digital camera that takes movies at 32 frames per second and has the capacity to film continuously), a scanner, and a $50 budget for software, your students can do blue-screen or green-screen digital storytelling, claymation, historical/interactive PowerPoint presentations with video and still photos, and more. Most impoverished schools we visit have the above hardware/software or better at their disposal. If not, don't hesitate to ask to borrow what you need from your district's central office, the nearest university, rotary club members, the local arts council, and community foundations. Invite the lenders (often they become donors) to come and watch your students' final presentations. You might be surprised how generous your community can be.

➤ **Lack of know-how.** Teachers are very, very busy. They often don't have the time to keep up on the latest hardware and software. But you don't have to be a techie to do digital storytelling. Your students are already masters at it—or will learn it with your encouragement. We further suggest encouraging your students to teach you and their fellow students what they know about how to operate and use the technological resources you have at your disposal. Your students will be your best instructors—they almost certainly know more than you, they have the time and motivation to keep up on what's new and available, and they are usually excellent instructors who feel proud and useful in helping you teach your class. So put them to work! Encourage them and thank them for their assistance.

Assign a student or a pair of students to teach others how to use the camera. Others can instruct on using microphones, the scanner, iMovie (comes free with Apple computers), or Movie Maker software. It is your job to facilitate their learning, give them time and access to learn how to use technology, and show them a thing or two about teaching (instead of just *telling* their fellow students how to do something, students should *model* it and then watch as their peers do it in guided practice). You can spend your time working with the individuals who need help and being the overall project manager while your students are hard at work creating interesting, worthwhile projects you and your community can be proud of.

Index of Suggested Stories by Story Type

- **Cumulative tales** use repetition, accumulation, rhythm, and a bare-bones plot to tell an entertaining story ("The Twelve Days of Christmas," "There Was an Old Lady Who Swallowed a Fly," "The House That Jack Built," and "The Little Red Hen," which is a musical cumulative tale).
- **Humorous tales, noodlehead stories, or trickster tales** are about a silly or stupid person who nevertheless wins out in the end ("Lazy Jack," "Brer Rabbit," and "Anansi the Spider").
- **Talking beast stories or fables** are about animals and creatures who talk just as humans do. Generally, they teach a lesson such as the rewards of courage, ingenuity, and independence ("The Three Little Pigs," "The Three Billy Goats Gruff," and "The Little Red Hen").
- **Magic tales or fairy tales** contain elements of magic or enchantment in characters, plot, or setting. Fairies, wizards, witches, talking mirrors, magic kisses, and enchanted forests are common in these stories ("Little Red Riding Hood," "Sleeping Beauty," and "Aladdin and the Wonderful Lamp").
- **Porquoi or creation tales** explain phenomena of nature. The word *porquoi* is French for *why*. These stories answer questions like *Why do the sun and moon live in the sky?* and *Why do mosquitoes buzz in people's ears?*
- **Realistic stories** deal with characters, plots, and exaggeration, but there is no magic involved ("Dick Whittington and His Cat" and "Bluebeard").

Cumulative Tales

Aardema, Verna. *Bringing the Rain to Kapiti Plain*. Puffin, 1992. Ages 4–8.

Andrews-Goebel, Nancy. *The Pot That Juan Built*. Illustrated by David Diaz. Lee & Low Books, 2002. Ages 5–10.

Arnold, Tedd. *There was an Old Lady Who Swallowed Fly Guy*. Scholastic, 2007, Ages 4–8.

Aylesworth, Jim. *The Gingerbread Man*. Scholastic, 1998. Ages 4–8.

Brett, Jan. *Berlioz the Bear*. Putnam Juvenile,1996. Ages 4–8.

Carle, Eric. *Today is Monday*. Putnam Juvenile,1997. Ages 4–8.

Wood, Audrey. *The Napping House: Book and Musical CD*. Illustrated by Don Wood. Harcourt Children's Books, 2004. Ages 4–8.

Humorous, Noodlehead Stories, or Trickster Tales

DeSpain, Pleasant. *Tales of Nonsense & Tomfoolery*. August House, 2001. Ages 4–8.

Hamilton, Martha and Weiss, Mitch. *Noodlehead Stories: World Tales Kids Can Read and Tell*. August House., 2000. Ages 6–11.

Hamilton,Virginia. *A Ring of Tricksters : Animal Tales from America, the West Indies, And Africa*. Illustrated by Bary Moser. Blue Sky Press, 1997. Ages 8–12.

McDermott, Gerald. *Zomo the Rabbit: A Trickster Tale from West Africa*. Voyager Books, 1996. Ages 4–8.

Souci, San Robert. *Sister Tricksters: Rollicking Tales of Clever Females*. August House, 2006. Ages 9–12.

Walker, Richard. *The Barefoot Book of Trickster Tales*. Illustrated by Claudio Muñoz. Barefoot Books, 1998. Ages 9–12.

Porquoi/Creation Tales

Aardena, Verna. *Why Mosquitoes Buzz in People's Ears*. Illustrated by Leo and Diane Dillon. Dial 1975. Ages 5–7.

Bruchac, Joseph, & James Bruchac. *How Chipmunk Got His Stripes: A Tale of Bragging and Teasing*. Illustrated by Jose Aruego and Arlane Dewey. Dial, 2001. Ages 5–8.

Bryan, Ashley. *The Story of Lightning and Thunder*. Aladdin, 1999. Ages 5–9.

Hamilton. Virginia. *In the Beginning: Creation Stories from around the World*. Illustrated by Barry Moser. Harcourt Paperbacks, 1991. Ages 12 and up.

Mayo, Margaret. *When the World Was Young: Creation and Pourquoi Tales*. Illustrated by Louise Brierley. Simon & Schuster Children's Publishing,1996. Ages 9–12.

Rosen, Michael and John Clemenstson. *How Animals Got Their Colors: Animal Myths From Around the World*. Harcourt Brace, 1992. Ages 9 and up.

Strauus, Kevin. *Tales with Tails: Storytelling the Wonders of the Natural World*. Libraries Unlimited, 2006. Ages 9 and up.

Magic Tales or Fairy Tales

Grimm, Wilhelm and Jacob Grimm. *The Complete Grimm's Fairy Tales*. CreateSpace, 2008. Ages 6–12.

Clark, Margaret. *The Very Best of Aesop's Fables*. Illustrated by Charlotte Voake. Walker Books Ltd, 2009. Ages 4–9.

Gavin, Jamilia. *The Whistling Monster: Stories from Around the World*. Walker Books Ltd, 2009. Ages 9–12.

Goodall, Jane. *The Eagle and the Wren*. Illustrated by Alexander Reichstein. North-South, 2002. Ages 5–8.

Lobel, Arnold. *Fables*. Harper, 1980. Ages 4-8.

Mandela, Nelson, editor. *Nelson Mandela's Favorite African Folktales*. W. W. Norton, 2007. Ages 9–12.

Scieska, John. *The True Story of the Three Little Pigs by A. Wolf*, Illustrated by Lane Smith.Viking, 1989. Ages 7–12.

White, E. B. *Charlotte's Web*. Illustrated by Grath Williams. Harper,1952. Ages 8–11.

Realistic Stories/Historical Fiction

Bunting, Eve. *Train to Somewhere*. Illustrated by Ronald Himler. Sandpiper, 2000. Ages 4–8.

Cushman, Karen. *Catherine, Called Birdy*. Harper Trophy, 1995. Ages 12 and up.

Park, Linda Sue. *The Firekeeper's Son*. Illustrated by Julie Downing

Sandpiper, 2009. Ages 4–8.

Peck, Richard. *On The Wings of Heroes*. Puffin, 2008. Ages 9–12.

Ritter, John. *The Desperado Who Stole Baseball*. Philomel, 2009. Ages 9–12.

Turner, Ann. *Mississippi Mud: Three Prairie Journals*. Illustrated by Robert Blake. Harper Collins, 1997. Ages 4–8.

Zarian, Beth Barteson. *Around the World with Historical Fiction and Folktales: Highly Recommended and Award-Winning Books*. The Scarecrow Press, Inc., 2004. Ages 5–12.

Performance Literacy through Storytelling

Bibliography

Aristotle (1951). *Poetics.* (S. H. Butcher, Trans., 4th ed.) New York: Dover Publications. (Original work published 350 B.C.).

Bishop, K., & Kimball. M. A. (2006). Engaging students in storytelling. *Teacher Librarian, 33(4),* 28-31.

Black, J. (2008). Why bother: the use of storytelling in the classroom. *Stories in Education.* Retrieved March 16, 2008 from http://www.storiesalive.com/ education/bother.htm.

Bower, G. H. (1978). Experiments on story comprehension and recall. *Discourse Processes, 1,* 211-231.

Boyce, J. S., Alber-Morgan, & Riley, J. G. (2007). Fearless public speaking: Oral presentation activities for the elementary classroom. *Childhood Education, 83(3),* 142-150.

Chesin, G. A. (1966). Storytelling and storyreading. *Peabody Journal of Education, 43(4),* 212-214.

Cummins, J. (2007). Pedagogies for the poor? Realigning reading instruction for low-income students with scientifically based reading research. *Educational Researcher, 36* (6), 564-572.

Cutspec, P. A. (2006). Oral storytelling within the context of the parent-child relationship. *Talaris Research Institute, 1(2),* 1-8.

Dillingham, B. (2005). Performance literacy. *The Reading Teacher,* 59(1), 72-76.

Durkin, R. & Jarney, M. (September, 2001). Staying after school—and loving it. *Principal Leadership, 2,* (1), 50-53.

Ellis, R. (2006). The spoken word. In Goss, L., Pritchett, D., & Reed, C. F. (Eds.), (2006). *Sayin' somethin': Stories from the National Association of Black Storytellers.* (pp. 97-98). Kearney, NE: Morris Publishing.

Feagans, L., & Appelbaum, M. I. (1986). Validation of language subtypes in learning disabled children. *Journal of Educational Psychology, 78(5),* 358-364.

Fisher, D., & Fry, N. (2007). Implementing a schoolwide literacy framework: Improving achievement in an urban elementary school. *The Reading Teacher, 6 (1)* 32-43.

Florida Department of Education (2007). *Reading/Language Arts Standards for Florida.* Retrieved from http://etc.usf.edu/flstandards/la/index.html.

Forest, H. (2002). Crafting personal vision in crafting folktales. *Story Arts Online*. Retrieved from http://www.storyarts.org/articles/vision.html.

Forest, H. (2006). The power of words: Leadership, metaphor, and story. *Story Arts Online*. Retrieved from http://www.storyarts.org/docs/The-Power-of-Words-Leadership-Metaphor-and-Story.pdf.

Forest, H. (2007). Heather Forest—Sharing musical folktales with young listeners. (In *The Art of Storytelling with Children*). Retrieved from http://www.storytellingwithchildren.com/?p=69#more-69.

Fox Eades, J.M. (2006). *Classroom tales: Using storytelling to build emotional, social, and academic skills across the primary curriculum.* London: Jessica Kingsley Publishers.

Gentner, D. R. (1976). The structure and recall of narrative prose. *Journal of Verbal Learning and Verbal Behavior, 15,* 411-418.

Groce, R. D. (2004). An experimental study of elementary teachers with the storytelling process: Interdisciplinary benefits associated with teacher training and classroom integration. *Reading Improvement, 41(2),* 122-129.

Hamilton, M., & Weiss, M. (1996). *Stories in my pocket: Tales kids can tell.* Golden, CO: Fulcrum Publishing.

Hardy, B. (1977). Narrative as a primary act of mind. In M.Meek, A. Warlow, & G. Barton (Eds.), *The cool web: The pattern of children's reading* (pp. 12-33). London: Bodley Head.

Heller, M. F. (2006/2007). Telling stories and talking facts: First graders; engagements in a nonfiction book club. *The Reading Teacher, 60(4), 358-369.*

Im, J., Parlakian, R., & Osborn, C.A. (2007). Stories: Their powerful role in early language and literacy. *Young Children, 62(1),* 52-53.

IRA/NCTE (2008). *Standards for the English language Arts*. Retrieved on March 18, 2008 from http://www.readwritethink.org/standards/index.html.

Ivey, B. (2008). *Arts, inc : How greed and neglect have destroyed our cultural rights. Berkeley: University of California Press.*

King, N. (2007). Developing imagination, creativity, and literacy through collaborative storymaking: A way of knowing. *Harvard Educational Review,* 77(2), 204-229.

Lynch-Brown, C., & Tomlinson, C.M. (2006). *Essentials of children's literature.* Boston: Pearson Education.

Mello, R. (2001, August 30-September 1). Building bridges: How storytelling influences Teacher/student relationships. Paper presented at the Storytelling in the Americas Conference, St. Catherine's, ON.

Mooney, B., & Holt, D. (Eds.). (1996). *The storyteller's guide: Storytellers share advice from the classroom, boardroom, showroom, podium, pulpit and center stage.* Little Rock, AR: August House Publishers.

National Reading Panel (2000). *Teaching children to read.* Washington, D.C.: National Institute of Health.

Nathanson, S. (2006). Harnessing the power of story: Using narrative reading and writing across the content areas. *Reading Horizons, 47* (1), 1-26.

NCTE (1992). Teaching storytelling: A position statement from the committee on storytelling. *NCTE Guideline.* Retrieved on March 18, 2008 from http://www.ncte.org/about/over/positions/category/lang/107637.htm?source=gs.

Norfolk, S., Stenson, J., & Williams, D. (2006). *The storytelling classroom: Applications across the classroom.* Westport, CN: Libraries Unlimited.

Ogle, D.M. (1986). K-W-L: A teaching model that develops active reading of expository text. *Reading Teacher, 39,* 564-570.

Ohler, J. (n.d.). Art of storytelling (Part II). *Digital and traditional storytelling.* Retrieved January 2009 from http://www.jasonohler.com/storytelling/storymaking.cfm.

Ohler, J. (2008.) Digital storytelling in the classroom: New media pathways to literacy, learning, and creativity. Thousand Oaks, CA: Corwin Press.

Palmer, B. C., Leiste, S.M., James, K.D., & Ellis, S.M. (2000). The role of storytelling in effective family literacy programs., *Reading Horizons, 41 (2),* 93-104.

Palmer, B.C., Harshbarger, S. J., & Koch, C.A. (2001). Storytelling as a constructivist model for developing language and literacy. *Journal of Poetry Therapy, 14 (4),* 199-212.

Peck, J. (1989). Using storytelling to promote language and literacy development. *The Reading Teacher, 43(2),* 138-141.

Peng, H., Fitzgerald, G., & Park, M. K. (2006). Producing multimedia stories with ESL Children: A partnership approach. *Journal of Educational Multimedia and Hypermedia, 15 (3),* 261-285.

Pink, D.H. (2005). *A whole new mind: Why right-brainers will rule the future.* New York: Riverhead Books.

Price, R. (1978). *A palpable God : Thirty stories translated from the Bible with an essay on the origins and life of narrative.* New York: Atheneum.

Roney, C. R. (1989). Back to the basics with storytelling. *The Reading Teacher, 42(7),* 520-523.

Rothlein, L., & Meinbach, A.L. (1966). *The world of books: Discovering good literature.* New York: HarperCollins Publishers.

Sanacore, J. (2004). Genuine caring and literacy learning for African American children. *The Reading Teacher, 57 (8),* 744-754.

Speaker, K.M., Taylor, D., & Kamen, R. (2004). Storytelling: Enhancing language acquisition in young children. *Education, 125(1),* 3-15.

Stadler, M. A. ,& Ward, G.C. (2005). Supporting the narrative development of young children. *Early Childhood Education Journal, 33(2),* 73-80.

Stanley, N. (2004). *Creating readers with poetry.* Gainesville, FL: Maupin House Publishing.

Starko, A.J. (2005). *Creativity in the classroom: Schools of delight* (3rd ed). Mahwah, NJ: *Lawrence Erlbaum Associates.*

Strickland, D. S., & Morrow, L. M. (1989). Young children's early writing development. *The Reading Teacher, 42(6),* 426-427.

Stuczynski, A., Linik, J.R., Novick, R., Spraker, J., Tucci, P., & Ellis, D. (2005). Tapestry of tales: Stories of self, family, and community provide rich fabric for *learning.* Portland, OR: Northwest Regional Educational Laboratory.

Wells, G. (1986). *The meaning makers.* Portsmouth, NH: Heinemann.

Wells, G. and Claxton, G. (Eds.) (2002). *Learning for life in the 21st century: Sociocultural perspectives on the future of education.* Oxford: Blackwell Publishers.

Wenner, J. A. (2004). Preschoolers' comprehension of goal structure in narratives. *Memory, 12,* 193-202.

Willingham, D. T. (2004). Ask the cognitive scientist: The privileged status of story. *American Educator, 28(2)* ,43-45;51-53.

Zinger, D. (2007, June 3). Employee engagement: Engage with stories. *David Zinger on employee management* (MMP #16). Retrieved from http://www.davidzinger. wordpress.com.

Audio CD Track List

(Total Time: 70 minutes)

Track Title	Lesson Page
1. **The Little Red Hen** (4:13) by Heather Forest. Performed by the author.	42
2. **Barn Dance** (3:43) by Bill Martin Jr. and John Archambault. Performed by John Archambault and David Plummer.	52
3. **Blizzard Wizard** (1:21) by Karen Alexander. Performed by the Nile Stanley and Ben Brenner.	58
4. **Patrick Gas, the Carpenter** (2:32) by Allan Wolf. Performed by the author.	74
5. **Raven Day** (7:06) by Brett Dillingham. Performed by the author.	60
6. **Billy and Harry** (7:20) by Brett Dillingham. Performed by the author.	69
7. **The Duck Who Ducked and Plucked** (3:06) by Brett Dillingham. Performed by the author.	50
8. **Sally and the Sea** (5:27) by Brett Dillingham. Performed by the author.	22
9. **The Hungry Crow** (1:44) by Brett Dillingham. Performed by the author.	44
10. **Barcomi and the Flying Dinosaur** (6:32) by Brett Dillingham. Performed by the author.	63
11. **The Things Willy Wumperbill Saw** (7:36) by Brett Dillingham. Performed by the author.	79
12. **How Drum Learned to Talk** (4:13) by Nile Stanley. Performed by Nile Stanley and Ben Brenner.	67
13. **The UnderToe** (1:06) by Karen Alexander. Performed by Nile Stanley and Ben Brenner.	58
14. **The Sleeping Sea** (0:54) by Karen Alexander. Performed by Nile Stanley and Ben Brenner.	54
15. **October 31st** (1:12) by Karen Alexander. Performed by Nile Stanley and Ben Brenner.	54
16. **Spudbuster** (2:44) by Nile Stanley and Ben Brenner. Performed by Nile Stanley and Ben Brenner.	90
17. **Hummingbird and Elephant** (7:15) by Brenda Hollingswoth-Marley. Performed by the author.	78
18. **I Am a Jinx** (3:08) by Jeff Trippe. Performed by the author.	86

About the Authors

Nile Stanley, Ph.D.

www.unf.edu/~nstanley/home.htm

Affectionately known as "Nile Crocodile, the Reading Reptile," Stanley is a performance poet, digital storyteller, researcher, and professor of reading and education at the University of North Florida. Nile is the author of the book *Creating Readers with Poetry* (2004). He is a former editor of the *Florida Reading Quarterly*, and a former president of the New Mexico State Council of the International Reading Association (IRA). He served as an evaluator for the Even Start early literacy project at Florida International University, Miami. Stanley has also been a professor-in-residence at Sallye B. Mathis Elementary School, Lake Forest Elementary School, and Brentwood Elementary School of the Arts (all in Jacksonville). He directs poetry clubs at J. Allen Axson Montessori School and St. Clair Evans Academy, which are supported by gifts from the Cummer Family Foundation. He uses poetry and storytelling to teach literacy to pre-kindergarten through fifth-grade students. UNF and Duval County Schools were the 2009 recipients of the National Association for Professional Development Schools Distinguished Program in Teacher Education and received a similar honor from the Association of Teacher Educators in 2003. Stanley is a frequent presenter at international, national, regional, state, and local conferences.

Brett Dillingham, M.Ed.

www.brettdillingham.com

Brett performs and teaches storytelling and performance literacy in Alaska, Canada, Ireland, England, Germany, Vietnam, Costa Rica, Nigeria, Russia, and the continental U.S. His work has been performed at the Kennedy Center for Performing Arts, and he has performed live storytelling on National Public Radio and at the Calgary International Children's Festival, Yukon Performing Arts Centre, National America Reads conference, National Migrant Education conference and the World Congress on Reading. He was selected to be the featured storyteller at the International Reading Association annual conference in 2005 and 2009. In his workshops, Brett teaches writing, storytelling, poetry and drama. He is the past president of the Alaska State Literacy Association (Alaska IRA) and is a published poet and playwright. His first children's book, *Raven Day*, was published in January 2002 by McGraw-Hill.